POLITICAL PHILOSOPHY
ALL THAT MATTERS

POLITICAL PHILOSOPHY

Johanna Oksala

ALL THAT MATTERS

ALL THAT MATTERS

First published in Great Britain in 2013 by Hodder & Stoughton. An Hachette UK company.

First published in US in 2013 by The McGraw-Hill Companies, Inc.

This edition published 2013

British Library Cataloguing in Publication Data: a catalogue record for this title is available from the British Library.

Library of Congress Catalog Card Number: on file.

10 9 8 7 6 5 4 3 2 1

The publisher has used its best endeavours to ensure that any website addresses referred to in this book are correct and active at the time of going to press. However, the publisher and the author have no responsibility for the websites and can make no guarantee that a site will remain live or that the content will remain relevant, decent or appropriate.

The publisher has made every effort to mark as such all words which it believes to be trademarks. The publisher should also like to make it clear that the presence of a word in the book, whether marked or unmarked, in no way affects its legal status as a trademark.

Every reasonable effort has been made by the publisher to trace the copyright holders of material in this book. Any errors or omissions should be notified in writing to the publisher, who will endeavour to rectify the situation for any reprints and future editions.

Typeset by Cenveo® Publisher Services.

Printed and bound in Great Britain by CPI Group (UK) Ltd., Croydon, CR0 4YY.

Hodder & Stoughton policy is to use papers that are natural, renewable and recyclable products and made from wood grown in sustainable forests. The logging and manufacturing processes are expected to conform to the environmental regulations of the country of origin.

Hodder & Stoughton Ltd

338 Euston Road

London NW1 3BH

www.hodder.co.uk

Also available in ebook

Contents

Introduction: What is political philosophy?

'Remember, if you please, that the man you call slave sprang from the same seed, enjoys the same daylight, breathes like you, lives like you, dies like you. You can as easily conceive him a free man as he can conceive you a slave.'

Seneca, *Essays and Letters*, p. 193

In doing the background reading for this book, I came across this eloquent passage in the writings of Seneca, the celebrated Roman philosopher and statesman. As you will see, Seneca is not included in the chapters of this short book. Nevertheless, I wanted to begin with him in order to illustrate the distinctive nature of political questions. The passage is striking because, while movingly exhorting us to recognize and respect the humanity of a slave, Seneca is not advocating the abolition of slavery – not at all; he sees nothing wrong with slavery as an institution. In other words, he approaches slavery as a moral and personal question of how we should treat people who appear different from us. He does not see slavery as a political problem – that is, a question concerning power relations and the justice of human organizations and institutions.

Seneca's thought also helps clarify two key contentions that have guided my approach to political philosophy in this book. The first is fairly simple: ideas matter. Many people interested in politics seem to think that while politics is essentially concerned with action – useful and practical tasks – political philosophy is just idle armchair speculation. What Seneca's example shows, however, is that if we are unable to *think* of slavery as a political problem, then we have no hope of even beginning to act for its abolition. The way we conceive and conceptualize social institutions, practices and human relations has direct consequences for our ability to organize politically and bring about change. In other words, political philosophy matters. Moreover, it matters to all of us because virtually everyone has to live in political relationships with other people.

My second point is more complex and involves the further question of what exactly political philosophy attempts to do. I have chosen to introduce political philosophy here mainly through a discussion of historical texts and figures. This might seem to be an odd approach to some people: many of the philosophers whose ideas I discuss have long been dead, and the world about which they philosophized no longer exists. You might wonder whether, in a short introduction such as this, it would not be better to extract these ideas and arguments from their historical contexts and focus on them only to the extent that they are still considered valid today.

However, in political philosophy, history is inseparable from the present. Significantly, politics happens in contexts that are historically situated, often changing dramatically over time. Unlike astrophysics or mathematics, there are no timeless, universal laws in political philosophy. The way we think about politics today is shaped directly by past events, and the concepts, ideas and arguments that we use to make sense of politics are necessarily inherited. Only an historical account makes it possible to understand them adequately.

There is another reason why I believe understanding something about the history of political thought is vital. I want to defend the view that one of the central objectives of political philosophy is to provide a critical perspective on our current political arrangements, organizations and power relations. We often fail to appreciate just how difficult this is. Seneca's thought illustrates this difficulty. Political philosophy is inevitably bound up with the social norms and cultural background beliefs of its time in ways that are difficult to untangle. If it were impossible for the Romans to see the profound injustice of the institution of slavery, is it not likely that we are just as blind to some deep political injustices in our society? Is it not probable that our thinking is limited in equally serious and fundamental ways?

I believe that an approach to political philosophy that introduces its key concepts and arguments as abstract and independent of historical context leads more easily to the problematic belief that these ideas are somehow inevitable and self-evident. Even a superficial understanding of history can shake such certitude, by showing how differently people have thought about political organizations and relationships in the past and, also, how recent some of our most cherished and taken-for-granted political principles are. Clearly for Seneca, it was far from self-evident that a society based on slavery fundamentally violates the principle that all humans have equal political rights. A great deal had to happen before anyone could formulate such a claim. First, the idea of a political right had to be conceived, and somehow people had to come around to believing that all human beings are equally capable and are entitled to be in charge of their lives.

I do not want to claim that the critical questioning of our taken-for-granted political beliefs and practices is the only task – or even the primary task – of political philosophy. As we will see in the course of this book, political philosophy also has other important objectives, a crucial one being simply to increase our understanding of the world around us. When we understand the ideas, arguments and debates that underpin our increasingly complex political problems, practices and institutions, it is much easier for us to act and orientate ourselves politically. It is also much easier to evaluate issues adequately. In politics, we are seldom satisfied merely with understanding political issues; we also want to make informed judgements about political decisions, forms of government and political objectives. Political philosophy offers systematic attempts to formulate criteria for making such evaluations. Political philosophy also engages in conceptual innovation. New conceptual tools, such as the idea of a 'political right' or 'the state', have allowed people to think in alternative and unprecedented ways about social organizations and political relationships, and this has made it possible for them to engage in new kinds of political action. Finally, political philosophy must also continuously engage in critical self-reflection and ask what politics and political philosophy mean. It is through such testing of the limits of our thought and practice that the sphere of politics can be radically contested, modified and expanded.

This book is an introduction, which should be understood in the original or literal sense of introduction as 'leading the way in'. Rather than attempting to provide a comprehensive and balanced overview, I hope to indicate entry points into political philosophy that readers can then pursue further. I do not intend to present any original arguments of my own or to defend my political views. However, I am well aware that my approach as well as my selection of what is included and what is excluded already tells a certain kind of story. If this story seems in some respects unorthodox, it is worth remembering that what characterizes contemporary political philosophy is the increasing acceptance that what is defined as 'political' has itself become an issue of political contestation. Along with traditional questions of political philosophy on the legitimacy of political authority or the merits of different constitutions, new and divisive topics have emerged, such as feminism, multiculturalism, indigenous peoples' rights, cyberspace, animal welfare, biotechnology and environmental issues. It is my contention that an introduction to political philosophy today means including some of these issues.

The book is divided into nine chapters and an epilogue. Each chapter focuses on selected classical texts in political philosophy, which are briefly introduced and analysed. These texts then function as a springboard for discussion of contemporary issues central to political philosophy. The texts move chronologically from antiquity to the twentieth century. We will be able to follow the historical development of certain political questions and ideas, but obviously I cannot provide a comprehensive history of political thought within this brief framework. The structure of the book is primarily thematic, and its focus is on contemporary political issues.

I strongly believe that there is no one right way to theorize about politics; rather, politics is a realm that can and should be approached from multiple perspectives and studied in various contexts. Hence, rather than attempting to provide a definite answer to the question of what political philosophy is, I invite you instead to consider many of the issues that we encounter every day as being political – as the outcome of human practices that incorporate power relations, social norms and obligations. I suggest that political philosophy be understood as an open-ended, critical project that concerns everyone; we should all engage in thinking about politics. And a good place to start is to step on board Plato's drunken pleasure cruise.

1

Democracy

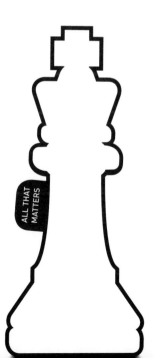

ALL THAT MATTERS

'Imagine the following situation on board a fleet of ships, or on a single ship. The captain has the edge over everyone else on board by virtue of his size and strength, but he's rather deaf and short-sighted, and his knowledge of naval matters is just as limited. The sailors are all wrangling with one another because each of them thinks that he ought to be the captain, despite the fact that he's never learned how, and can't name his teacher or specify the period of his apprenticeship. In any case, they all maintain that it isn't something that can be taught, and are ready to butcher anyone who says it is. They're for ever crowding closely around the captain, pleading with him and stopping at nothing to get him to entrust the rudder to *them. Sometimes, if their pleas are unsuccessful, but others get the job, they kill those others or throw them off the ship, subdue their worthy captain by drugging him or getting him drunk or something, take control of the ship, help themselves to its cargo, and have the kind of drunken and indulgent voyage you'd expect from people like that.'*

Plato, *Republic*, p. 208; translation slightly modified

Would you like to be the captain of a ship full of aggressive drunks who have no idea how to sail, but passionately argue that sailing requires no skill and that anyone can do it equally well? You probably wouldn't, yet you are just as likely to be a firm believer in democracy as the self-evident best form of government. Its value is taken for granted today to such an extent that it has almost become a vacuous term of praise rather than a definition of a political system in which people govern themselves collectively. For Plato (*c.*427–347 BCE), however, democracy is that ship of fools. While political philosophers often pride themselves on Western civilization's love of democracy, the inaugural text of the tradition of Western political thought, Plato's *Republic*, is its uncompromising critique.

The context of Plato's critique of democracy was the Athenian city-state, which during his lifetime experienced turbulent political upheavals such as a long war, oligarchic coups and the violent restoration of democracy. Perhaps the single most influential event for Plato's political thinking was the execution of Socrates, his beloved teacher and mentor. Socrates was charged with showing impiety towards the city's gods and for corrupting the youth of Athens with his philosophy. He was convicted by a democratic court, the majority of a jury of 501 citizens. Perhaps unsurprisingly, Plato's political thought emphasizes the importance of the unity

▲ The Platonic metaphor of the 'ship of state' has reverberated through history, here used in an American political cartoon from the early nineteenth century.

and stability of political order and, as we have seen from the extract above, he severely mistrusts the ability of the people to make informed political judgements or to know what is good for them.

The *Republic* is sometimes dismissed as an evil treatise for tyrants because of its depiction of democracy as chaotic mob rule. Yet Plato's arguments against democracy remain worthy of serious consideration. Even if we strongly disagree with him, his arguments should prompt us to think about why we believe in democracy so strongly. It should also be borne in mind that Plato engages in a radical project of political imagination. Thus, we should not be stuck in debating whether or not his ideas are feasible. The philosopher is not a politician, nor is she constantly faced with practical problems that demand immediate decisions and difficult compromises. Instead, she can describe ideals against which our actual political arrangements can be shown to be inadequate in some respect. At times, she must also attempt to imagine the unimaginable: to open up radically new political horizons and avenues of thought. Plato's political vision might be outlandish and unfeasible, but we must give him credit for thinking outside the social conventions of his society instead of just replicating them. When he argued that women as well as men could become rulers and that they should receive exactly the same education for the job as men, the claim was so outlandish as to be considered ridiculous. Whereas Plato's contemporary and student Aristotle argued that the souls of women and slaves were essentially different from those of free men and that this justified their subordination and exclusion from politics, Plato's emphasis was on the right kind of education. History shows that sometimes the most seemingly ridiculous political ideas eventually become the most celebrated.

Plato's key claim is that the governance of a political community demands the kind of professional skill, special knowledge and long training required of sailing. The true navigator must study the weather, read maps and have practical knowledge of steering a ship. Plato also makes a persuasive comparison to medicine: if you are ill, you would want to see a qualified doctor who had studied medicine for many years. You would hardly turn to a crowd and ask them to vote on the correct remedy. Hence, democracy is a dangerous idea for the simple reason that it gives the right to rule to those who are unqualified for it. Plato considers it as self-evident that you would be willing to obey someone who has the authority of knowledge, and, problematically, he also assumes that knowledge in the realm of politics is no different from the knowledge required for navigation or medicine.

Plato also insists that democracy is structurally unstable, regardless of the professional knowledge and moral intentions of its rulers. It necessarily results in warped decisions because democratically elected leaders have to sustain their popularity. They depend on the popular vote, which means that they will inevitably avoid unpopular decisions – think of how budget cuts are never announced before an election, for example. No matter how honest and upright people are, they will soon discover that they have to lie or keep quiet about unpleasant truths to remain in power. In short, Plato's concern was that, if people are allowed to decide on political matters, they will inevitably listen to those who look the best, shout the loudest and promise the most.

▶ Plato's ideal society

Despite the problems of democracy, most people consider Plato's alternative to be either completely unfeasible or so unappealing that they are prepared to stay aboard the perilous ship. To mention only some of the unsavoury features of Plato's alternative, he advocates a form of dictatorship that practises eugenics, imposes strict censorship on art and indoctrinates all workers into complete obedience.

In the *Republic* Plato describes an ideal society that perfectly mirrors the principle of justice, as he understands it. This society is built on a simple premise: individuals must adopt the role to which they are best suited. He divides people into three classes according to their natural talents and dispositions; these classes can be roughly described as rulers, soldiers and workers. Inborn talents are then complemented with a suitable education that optimally prepares the individuals for their future roles. Only those with superior intellect, moral virtue and the right kind of education are allowed to rule.

The life of the rulers, or guardians as Plato calls them, is not a life of luxury and privilege. Unlike workers, guardians are not allowed to own property, and they are forced to go to extremes to avoid the temptations of personal wealth:

> *they are not permitted to have any contact or involvement with gold or silver: they are not to come under the same roof as gold and silver, or wear them on their bodies, or drink from gold and silver cups. These precepts will guarantee not only their own integrity but also the integrity of the community which is in their safe keeping.'*

(Plato, *Republic*, pp. 121–2)

Nor can guardians have wives or children of their own. The abolition of family and female equality and the outlawing of personal wealth are all means of ruling out partisan interests, which would lead to corruption and dissent. Guardians must devote their lives exclusively to the common good: they must live communally and regard one another as belonging to an enormous, extended family.

It is also important to observe that what ultimately distinguishes the guardians from the other classes is not their superior intellect, but their superior moral understanding. Their modern equivalent would not be an Oxbridge-educated elite with doctorates in political science, for example. For Plato, virtue is a kind of knowledge: being a virtuous person means to understand 'the good'. Similar to an expert mathematician who knows the fundamental mathematical theorems and is then able to prove results with those, a philosopher knows the essence of moral truths and is able to apply this knowledge to political decisions. The long-term educational programme of the guardians would primarily be a moral, philosophical education. The guardians would be philosophers in Plato's sense of the word: individuals who are not interested in power, wealth or social status because for them happiness consists of knowing the truth. They would practise philosophy as a spiritual way of life, not as a career or a course of study.

Hence, Plato's citizens are clearly very different from us: they are not the modern, multitalented, dissenting individuals who believe that they can freely choose among different occupations and political arrangements according to their interests and preferences. For Plato, there is a natural, cosmic order to which societies as well as individuals must conform in order to live a good life. A political community is not just an aggregate of individuals, but an organic unity, like the human body, the different parts of which have to perform different functions for the whole to stay healthy.

▶ Modern and ancient democracies

Although we have inherited our idea of democracy from ancient Greece, ancient political thought is based on a very different worldview from our current political theories, and modern democracy differs from ancient democracy in many crucial respects. As we will see in the course of this book, in modern democracies the principle of the rule of the people is intertwined with a number of other important and specifically modern political ideas, namely that democracy takes place in a nation-state, it is linked to a specific mode of production – advanced capitalism – and its rationale is not the morally superior life of the community, but individual freedom and equality.

Modern and ancient democracies also represent two different types of democracy. In a *direct democracy* such as Athenian democracy, people vote for or against laws or policies rather than for candidates. By contrast, modern democracies are *representative democracies*: people vote for representatives who then make decisions for them. Many contemporary critics of parliamentary democracy therefore argue that what we call *democracy* is in fact an *oligarchy*, the rule of a wealthy elite. To become an electoral candidate usually requires substantial fund-raising as well as marketing, branding and advertising, causing the majority of citizens to be turned into passive bystanders in an electoral spectacle. Voter turnout in parliamentary elections in many Western countries has been steadily declining and at times has reached alarmingly low levels. This raises the serious question of whether today the elected representatives can in fact be seen as actually representing the people.

Despite the clear differences from ancient democracy, modern democracies, critics suggest, also come much closer to Plato's view than we like to admit. While we proclaim that everyone is equally qualified to make political decisions and that in a democracy no one has any special entitlement to exercise power, in modern democracies there is a fundamental tendency and a silent acceptance that certain political decisions should be left to experts. Economic decisions and military decisions are perhaps the most obvious examples. Economic decisions are increasingly insulated from parliamentary decision-making and allocated to central banks and financial institutions. Military decisions are classified as sensitive national security matters and are made by specifically trained military personnel with no direct democratic mandate. The reluctance of most European countries to hold popular referenda on the constitution of the European Union (EU) was sometimes seen as another rendition of the drunken cruise: ignorant people sabotaging important political processes by being misled by whimsical interests and populist politicians.

The remedies suggested for dealing with the problems of democracy also turn on the issues raised by Plato. Like Plato, many political thinkers emphasize the role of the right education in politics. They argue that such education is a precondition for a functioning democracy: people must have sufficient knowledge and understanding of politics in order to be motivated and to make informed decisions on the complex political issues that affect them. Some contemporary political thinkers have also attempted to rethink the crucial dichotomy underlying Plato's political thought – randomness versus a true order. In opposition to Plato, they argue that randomness should be affirmed as the basis of politics. Their contention is that *aleatory democracy* – a form of democracy in which representatives for certain political positions are decided by lottery – would effectively eliminate several forms of bias from politics because pure chance is incorruptible. It would eliminate dependence on the media and campaign donors and do away with populist promises and dishonesty, elitism and exclusivity. It could also remedy voter cynicism and apathy, since all citizens would have to be prepared to navigate the ship in their turn. In ancient democracies, choosing representatives for certain positions by lottery was a common practice. The fact that today we tend to think of aleatory democracy as a strange idea suggests that perhaps we are more in agreement with Plato than we like to acknowledge. If everyone is equally able and entitled to make political decisions, then why should a political leader not be selected from volunteers by lottery?

Democracy, as we currently know and practise it, is thus only one form that the idea of power-sharing by the people can take. The idea of democracy itself does not necessarily imply politicians, representation, parliaments, free markets, constitutions or nation-states, for example. Nor does it specify what the powers are that must be shared by the people or how the rule of the people should be organized. In the chapters that follow, a host of additional ideas will be introduced and discussed in order to illustrate how we have come to live in contemporary liberal democracies and why we regard them as the best political systems. We also have to consider the serious challenges that globalization presents for democratic decision-making as well as assess the principles that are required to stop democracy from turning into a tyranny of the majority. But first we have to address the vital question of who the people – the *demos* in the word 'democracy' – really are.

Political animals

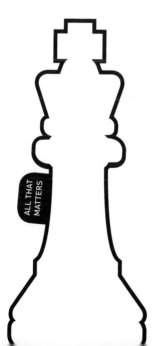

'It follows that the state belongs to the class of objects which exists by nature, and that man is by nature a political animal... But obviously man is a political animal in a sense in which a bee is not, or any other gregarious animal. Nature, as we say, does nothing without some purpose; and she has endowed man alone among the animals with the power of speech. Speech is something different from voice, which is possessed by other animals also and used by them to express pain or pleasure; for their nature does indeed enable them not only to feel pleasure and pain, but to communicate these feelings to each other. Speech, on the other hand, serves to indicate what is useful and what is harmful, *and so also what is just and what is unjust. For the real difference between man and other animals is that humans alone have perception of good and evil, just and unjust, etc. It is the sharing of a common view on these matters that makes a household and a state.'*

Aristotle, *Politics*, pp. 59–60

Aristotle's *Politics* (*c.*350 BCE) is a difficult and rambling book: a series of topics examined, discarded and re-examined from another perspective. It is likely that the form in which we read the text today is not the one intended by Aristotle. The books and chapters might have been in a different sequence, and they were probably written at different times for different purposes. Yet the book is one of the key texts of Western political thought, and it inaugurated a completely new approach to the study of politics.

Aristotle is highly sceptical of the value of utopian political thought and abstract philosophical speculation, and he emphasizes the importance of empirical knowledge: we need to observe carefully and analyse the world around us in order to understand politics. For him, political philosophy cannot be solely a prescriptive discipline attempting to lay out the organization of the ideal state; it must also be able to provide descriptive analyses of the actual facts of politics. Aristotle does indeed conduct an analysis of the ideal constitution – the ancient political philosopher's traditional topic – and provides a qualified defence of democracy, but he also engages in a detailed and comparative study of existing and past constitutions and draws conclusions about the ways in which they are likely to develop. For Aristotle, the best form of government is a *polity*, a mixed government that combines elements from the institutions of democracy and oligarchy. Yet it is important to observe that this is not the ideal government, but only the 'best in the circumstances' and practically achievable (p. 236).

One can hear the sarcasm in his words and imagine that they were directed at Plato when he writes: 'We can in our speculations postulate any ideal conditions we like, but they should at least be within the limits of possibility' (p. 122). He also has a sharp eye for the practical difficulties in Plato's plan, noting the problems that follow from communal living; for example:

> *People are much more careful of their personal possessions than of those owned communally.... Each citizen acquires a thousand sons, but these are not one man's sons; any one of them is equally the son of any other person, and as a result will be equally neglected by everyone (p. 108).*

▶ Being a citizen

The most famous line in Aristotle's *Politics* is the one in which he claims that man is a 'political animal' (p. 59).

But what exactly does he mean by this and what are the consequences of this claim for our understanding of politics? The idea implies that man is an animal like other non-human animals and therefore has a natural way of life that is optimal for the species. Human beings are animals who naturally seek to live together, but they are distinct from all other animals in the crucial respect that only they are political beings, capable of making moral distinctions between good and evil and between the just and the unjust.

Similar to Plato's, Aristotle's political thought is inseparable from the ethical question of the highest good for human beings and how this can be achieved. He insists that humans do not aim merely to survive, as do other animals; they aim to live a good life – a life of happiness and moral virtue. Such a life is possible only as a citizen, as an active participant in a political community. Not to take part in politics, in the ruling of the political community together with other citizens, would mean not exercising the highest rational and moral faculties that man possesses. It would mean living like a slave or an animal: without virtue or honour. Aristotle also condemns the idea that a citizen should devote all his time to the acquisition of wealth. Wealth has no intrinsic value and can only contribute to the pursuit of the good life in moderation. A political association does not exist so that people can live a safe and materially comfortable life; it exists 'for the sake of noble actions' (p. 198). In other words, it exists so that people can contribute their talents and ideas to the political project of building a common world in which they can flourish and live a good life. Aristotle's message is uncompromising: to live a life worthy of a human being means engaging in the political life of one's community.

This idea should give some pause to modern readers. While the idea is often celebrated as underlying our civic tradition, how many of us can really say that we live a good life in Aristotle's sense by taking an active part in the building of our political communities? Do our modern political systems even make such participation possible by providing sufficient opportunities? Or does the hectic, modern lifestyle simply leave most of us too isolated and too busy to become engaged in complex political issues?

Aristotle recognizes that politics is an activity that demands time and appropriate knowledge and it therefore requires education and a certain amount of leisure. His affirmation of a truly human life as the goal of politics therefore also erects a problematic boundary of exclusion that demands some critical scrutiny.

▶ The boundaries of democracy

The population of Athens in the fifth century BCE is estimated to have been around 250,000 people, but, of those, only about 30,000 had the political rights of a citizen. Women, slaves, foreign residents and others who did not meet the strict lineage requirements for citizens were excluded from politics. Citizenship thus functioned

▲ The hill known as the Pnyx was the meeting place for the popular assembly of ancient Athens. While modern Western democracy is often traced back to the Athenian political system, the assembly at the Pnyx excluded the large majority of the Athenian population, women and slaves included.

as a stark measure for separating those entitled to lead a political, truly human life from those who lacked this possibility, and politics was understood and defined through this exclusion. Some people had to provide the necessities of life – food, water, houses, roads and so on – in order for the citizens to have the opportunity to engage in politics and in public deliberation and debate in juries and assemblies.

The principles of exclusion in ancient Greece were thus fairly extreme, and we are rightfully appalled by their limited understanding of democratic equality. But it is important to acknowledge that principles of exclusion are inherent in our modern democracies as well. For us, the *demos* – the people who rule themselves – is defined through national citizenship, which is the basis of our political rights. Modern democracies also contain people who live among us and who often materially help sustain our way of life, but who do not have the political rights of a citizen. These people are more numerous than we like to think: asylum seekers, foreign residents both legal and illegal, the seriously ill, the mentally handicapped, prisoners and children.

Our economy does not depend on the institution of slavery, yet even in Western democracies there are people working in slave-like conditions. It has been estimated that in the EU countries alone there are hundreds of thousands of victims of human trafficking, the majority of whom are women working in the sex industry. There are also numerous illegal immigrants who have arrived of their own accord in search of a decent standard of living and who provide cheap services and labour. One of the most pressing political issues today remains the question of who is entitled to take part in political decision-making processes and how the boundaries of our democracies are defined and secured.

It can also be argued that there are millions among us who lack even the minimal political protections of illegal immigrants, but who provide the necessary raw materials for our economies: I am referring to non-human animals. Animals provide food and raw materials for various industries, as well as contributing to the circulation of water and waste. In recent years the idea that animals should have some basic rights guaranteeing a life free of suffering and typical of their species has gained ground, and several political parties have been founded in different countries that attempt to represent animals politically.

We will see in the chapters that follow how both of these ideas – political rights and representation for animals – fundamentally challenge some of the key assumptions in the tradition of Western political thought. Political rights are traditionally understood as a result of a contract into which people enter. Such a contract imposes certain duties in return for rights. As animals cannot make contracts or perform duties, their political rights must be understood in a fundamentally different way. Whereas the idea of political representation is based on the idea that different groups elect their own representatives to advocate and defend their interests, political parties for animals, by contrast, are based on the principle of altruism: politics is not about advancing one's own interests, but the interests of those who are unable to represent themselves.

Environmental politics has recently begun to challenge anthropocentric politics more generally – the idea that politics aims solely at human improvement. While at one time environmentalists were dismissed in mainstream politics as irrational romantics advocating an unrealistic return to nature, today the tables have turned: denying or ignoring the importance of environmental questions has become the irrational position. We have reached a tipping point in regard to environmental issues such as climate change, pollution and the exploitation of resources, in the wake of which environmental politics has become an acute question of human survival, not merely a matter of lifestyle. It has now become apparent to most people that the environmental destruction caused by humans has to be addressed politically in order for *any* living being to survive, never mind flourish.

Biopolitics

Aristotle's famous distinction between animal life and political life has also been challenged in other fundamental ways in contemporary political thought. In the 1970s the French philosopher Michel Foucault (1926–1984) introduced the influential idea of biopolitics in his writings and argued that it overturned the ancient categories of biological and political existence. Modern politics no longer excludes biological life the way Aristotle did. Instead, human biological life has become the primary object of modern politics – an object of intense political calculation and governance.

Foucault contends that the political power exercised over modern citizens is no longer primarily repressive, but has a different rationality. The purpose of modern biopolitics is to regulate and optimize life: it attempts to ensure that people live longer and are healthier by regulating their dietary habits, for example. This is accomplished not only with the traditional instruments of politics such as laws, but also through the imposition of habits and norms. Biopolitics collects increasingly detailed statistical and medical information about a population and establishes optimal standards: scientific discourses tell us the normal weight, blood pressure and number of sexual partners for a certain gender and age group, for example. We modify our behaviours in an endless attempt to approximate the norm and in the process become a certain kind of political subject. Biopolitics is thus an effective form of social control that takes over the management of individual lives from before birth until death. Larger and larger areas of life are medicalized in today's society and thereby brought under bio-scientific control.

In sum, Aristotle challenges us to question the idea that the value of democracy is merely instrumental. Most of us would probably admit that often democracy is not a particularly effective means for achieving political solutions. Nor should democracy be defended primarily with abstract political principles such as the autonomy and equality of citizens. Instead, its chief value lies in the fact that democratic political participation is essential for human self-realization and wellbeing. Modern democracies' exclusion of others, however, as well as the increasing importance of biopolitics, effectively undermines this ideal. Not everybody seems to be able to take part equally in such self-realization and wellbeing, nor does self-realization seem to be a viable goal any longer in modern biopolitical societies – in which thriving as a human being is equated merely with biological survival, longevity and the health of the general population. In addition to these challenges, I also anticipate that, after all this emphasis on self-realization and noble actions, some of you may be ready to raise the objection advanced by my next interlocutor: Isn't it naive to believe that real politics has anything to do with noble actions?

3

Secrets and lies

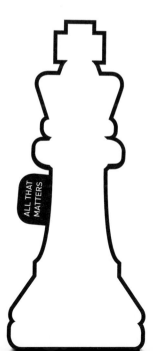

'Many have dreamed up republics and principalities which have never in truth been known to exist; the gulf between how one should live and how one does live is so wide that a man who neglects what is actually done for what should be done moves towards self-destruction rather than self-preservation. The fact is that a man who wants to act virtuously in every way necessarily comes to grief among so many who are not virtuous. Therefore if a prince wants to maintain his rule he must be prepared not to be virtuous, and to make use of this or not according to need.'

Machiavelli, *The Prince*, p. 65

The Prince by Niccolò Machiavelli (1469–1527) is one of the most controversial books on political philosophy ever written, and the name Machiavelli has become synonymous with political nihilism: the idea that there is no moral basis for politics. Politics aims solely for the attainment of power for the sake of power. To describe a politician as 'Machiavellian' has come to mean that he or she is a cunning, an amoral and an opportunistic individual. While even the most ruthless politicians refuse to be associated with his name, Machiavelli's innovations in political thought are nevertheless undeniable.

▶ Power play

Both Plato and Aristotle believed that political philosophy was a form of knowledge just like biology or geometry: with it, one could discover objective or absolute truths. For these philosophers, political questions were also inseparable from ethics. Political thought was pointless if it could not reveal something about how to live a good life. Machiavelli's *The Prince* is based on completely different premises: there are no objective moral truths in politics, and political success therefore requires skill, not knowledge. We all know that it is impossible for everyone to win in a game. Just as we cannot decide who should win a football match through scientific or moral debate, so in the political contest for power we can find out the winner only by playing the game and seeing which player is the most skilful.

Machiavelli was born in Florence, a prosperous Italian city-state and one of the main centres of Renaissance art and scholarship. The Europe of Machiavelli's time was an unstable mix of principalities ruled by princes, counts and dukes from whose realms the modern nation-states of Europe would slowly emerge. There were constant wars as well as uprisings, political intrigues and assassinations. Machiavelli observed these events first-hand, as he held a series of political positions in Florence and travelled widely across Italy and southern Europe on diplomatic missions. It was this practical knowledge of 'statecraft', as well as his thorough study of the history of Rome, that he drew on in his political thinking.

Two major upheavals in European political thought separate Machiavelli from Plato and Aristotle: Roman political ideas and Christianity. Political thought in medieval Europe was dominated by Christian doctrine, which strongly rejected the ancient emphasis on the importance of politics as essential for the good life. True happiness could no longer be achieved in this world, it was believed, but was the reward granted after death for all eternity. Political conquests – fame, riches and power – were fleeting and fortuitous, while the Christian values of meekness and humility led to eternal rewards.

However, with the recovery of classical Roman political ideals in the Renaissance, the attainment of glory as the highest human achievement resurfaced. In this respect, Machiavelli follows Roman political thinkers. He takes it for granted that men desire glory and riches above all else, and a main objective of *The Prince* is to tell the readers how to achieve these goals.

▲ Niccolò Machiavelli – Renaissance bogeyman or political realist?

While the classical Roman philosophers had argued that moral virtue was indispensable to political success, Machiavelli's original and provocative move was to divorce the two. If a ruler wanted to maintain his rule and obtain glory, then it was complete folly to be morally upright. Politics was a strategic and ruthless game played by unscrupulous men. A ruler who tried to play the game by doing good was sure to lose. Machiavelli insisted that a great ruler had to be able to rise above ordinary morality, in the sense that he had to know when the circumstances demanded moral rectitude and when they demanded the opposite: secrecy, deception, war and cunning.

Hence, the fundamental lesson about politics that Machiavelli teaches is that politics is not a debate club – it is a contest for power. In politics the only rule is that there are no rules, because every political situation is different and its outcome unpredictable. Only a ruler who understands this and is flexible enough to adapt to changing circumstances will be successful. Machiavelli's approach to politics thus seems to be purely strategic and devoid of any moral consideration at all.

▶ Ends and means

If we study Machiavelli's thought more closely, however, we see that his position is nuanced and complex. He is in fact not arguing for complete and utter amoral opportunism in which all means are equally permissible in the dog-eat-dog world of politics. He is also motivated by the Roman ideal of *patriotism*, the love of one's country, and argues that the seemingly immoral actions of a truly great ruler must be understood as exhibiting a deeper moral worth. He challenges all political idealists to consider not only whether it might at times be necessary to use immoral means in politics for lack of other options, but also whether using such means for worthy ends might in fact be the morally right thing to do.

When we think of politicians lying, we often think of someone like President Bill Clinton who, in a sworn deposition, lied about his relationship with Monica

Lewinsky in order to keep their affair a secret. It would seem that his action was textbook Machiavellian: he lied in order to hold on to power. But to understand Machiavelli's real argument, I suggest that it would be better to consider the actions of another president.

Risto Ryti

In the spring of 1944, after years of brutal war with the Soviet Union, the president of Finland, Risto Ryti, signed an agreement with the German foreign minister, Joachim von Ribbentrop, committing Finland to fight with Germany against the Soviet Union until the war's end. To sign such an agreement at that point in the Second World War was foolhardy because Germany's defeat was already obvious. However, the agreement was the condition Germany set for providing Finland with food and arms. Without this German military aid, the only option left for the Finns would have been unconditional surrender to the Soviet Union. The German aid helped Finland stop the advance of the Red Army during the summer of 1944, and when the peace negotiations started in August, Finland's position was much stronger. However, in order to pull out of the war and make peace with the Soviet Union, it was necessary to break the Ryti–Ribbentrop agreement. Because Ryti, a lawyer by training, had signed the agreement in his own name, he knew that legally the agreement obligated him alone and not his presidential successor. Thus, Ryti resigned, thereby dissolving the agreement, and the Moscow Armistice between Finland and the Soviet Union was signed on 19 September 1944.

Most Finns today believe that Ryti's cunning and deceit in signing a contract that he had no intention of honouring was the reason Finland managed to retain its independence and avoid Soviet occupation. Ryti's move was Machiavellian, not only because he decided that the situation demanded deception rather than honesty, but also, significantly, because he did not act deceitfully in order to advance his own interests, but the interests of his country. He signed knowing that, after breaking the agreement, he would probably be executed for his alliance with Germany in the war trials that followed the armistice. Although Machiavelli is often read as an advocate of individualistic opportunism, his reasons for advocating immoral action are ultimately for the greater good. A politician has to do what it takes to advance the welfare of the *patria*.

Machiavelli also acknowledges that, while a ruler cannot always avoid immoral actions, he should nevertheless not appear cruel, dishonest or immoral to his people. If the people hate him, then the ruler is on the surest route to losing his power and glory. It is thus necessary for a ruler to be a hypocrite: he must appear to be something that he is not and cannot be, namely morally upright. Hypocrisy is simply indispensable to good government. Yet, while Machiavelli counsels hypocrisy, he is anything but a hypocrite himself. Instead, he attempts to expose the unpleasant truths about politics that we would rather not see. He turns the tables on us: pretending that politics is a realm of honesty, moral rectitude and unadulterated altruism is a much more dangerous form of hypocrisy than accepting that secrets and lies are often necessary. Recognizing the true nature of politics enables us to engage in it with critical clarity: accepting that politicians have to lie sometimes will help us to expose some of the much greater lies that sustain our political beliefs and practices.

Machiavelli has become an important influence in contemporary political philosophy for theorists who hold that politics is always *agonistic*, or confrontational, because it is inevitably a struggle for power. Agonistic political theorists such as Chantal Mouffe, Bonnie Honig and William Connolly for example, insist that we have to accept that in post-traditional societies, which include people from diverse religious and ethnic groups, disagreements, conflicts and power struggles exist and cannot always be overcome through dialogue and education. These scholars argue that such acceptance can lead to fairer, more equal procedures for negotiating conflicts than pretending that a rational agreement can always be reached. Assuming that political practices are based on consensus often simply excludes individuals and groups by hiding their conflicting views. In other words, rather than taking for granted that political stability and consensus always reflect genuine agreement and harmony among individuals and groups, it is important to question whether instead it hides discord and disagreement behind a false façade.

Before we settle for the inevitability of conflict, however, we must consider the towering efforts in political philosophy to eradicate conflict – to free modern citizens and their political organizations from wars, revolts and instability. The obvious place to begin is the social contract – arguably the most influential political story of modern times. The social contract rests on the idea that all legitimate social and political relations must be based on rational consent and must take a contractual form.

4

The social contract

'Hereby it is manifest, that during the time men live without a common power to keep them all in awe, they are in that condition which is called war; and such a war is of every man against every man [...]. In such condition, there is no place for industry; because the fruit thereof is uncertain; and consequently no culture on earth; no navigation, nor use of the commodities that may be imported by sea; no commodious building; no instruments of moving, and removing such things as require much force; no knowledge of the face of the earth; no account of time; no arts; no letters; no society; and which is worst of all, continual fear, and danger of violent death;

and the life of man, solitary, poor, nasty, brutish, and short.'

Hobbes, *Leviathan*, pp. 91–2; slightly modernized

With Thomas Hobbes (1588–1679) we enter a distinctly modern political landscape, in which religious and traditional justifications of authority lose their credibility. His major work, *Leviathan* (1651), introduces and defends the celebrated and recognizably modern political idea that all men are born equal and free. Hobbes strongly denies Aristotle's claim that there is a natural hierarchy among human beings with some people inherently superior. Neither does he believe that men are political animals whose natural condition is to live together as participants in a political community. People are merely forced to live together out of fear of one another and the desire for self-preservation.

Hobbes lived during a period of intense intellectual revolution when the scientific ideas of Galileo Galilei and Isaac Newton were laying the foundations for a new mechanical and mathematical worldview and were stripping away the scholastic dogmas derived from Aristotle and the Bible. Hobbes wanted to adopt this new worldview to the study of politics. He was an unrelenting materialist; for him, human beings were nothing other than complex material objects similar to sophisticated robots. Their behaviour is therefore completely determined by natural egoism and the strong impulse of self-preservation, explainable through rigorous

Non est potestas Super Terram quæ Comparetur ei Iob. 41. 24.

LEVIATHAN
Or
THE MATTER, FORME
and Power of A COMMON-
WEALTH ECCLESIASTICALL
and CIVIL.

By THOMAS HOBBES
of MALMESBVRY.

London
Printed for Andrew Crooke
1651

▲ The famous frontispiece for *Leviathan* depicts the absolute ruler,
who alone, in Hobbes's opinion, can quell the rapacious egoism of
human nature.

scientific method. Significantly, Hobbes challenges the Christian doctrine that political power is handed down directly from God. In his view, kings do not rule by divine right. Political authority has to have a strictly rational basis to be acceptable to the modern scientific mind.

If we combine Hobbes's basic tenet that people are equal with his claim about the secular nature of political power, we can see how the central problem of modern political philosophy concerning the legitimacy of political authority emerges: Why should some people have the power to rule others? The political community is no longer a natural organization like a beehive. Neither does it reflect the will of God. Deeply rooted ideas, such as the idea that people are born into a preordained status and rulers reign by divine right, are replaced by the radical notion that all men are born free and equal. But if men really are free and equal, then why should they submit to the rule of others?

The answer provided by thinkers such as Hobbes, whom we today call social contract theorists, is that the only legitimate basis for political authority must be the voluntary consent of the people themselves. In other words, power cannot be forced on people; they have to agree to be ruled. All power relations must take a contractual form, and we must treat our political organizations as if they originated from a contract into which we have entered voluntarily. Social contract theory thus contributes to an enormous shift in political thought: modern politics becomes a realm of free and equal men making voluntary and rational choices and forming contractual relations among themselves.

▶ The state of nature

Hobbes invites us to perform a thought experiment. In order to understand the nature of political authority correctly, we must try to imagine a situation in which it does not exist. We must imagine 'a state of nature', a hypothetical situation defined by the lack of any kind of political authority. As the famous extract that opens this chapter shows, Hobbes's view of such a state of nature is grim: life would be nasty, brutish and short. In order to enter fully into the spirit of his thought experiment, it is best not to think of the state of nature as some kind of original or actual historical period that preceded known civilization. We should instead think of the period of the English Civil War (1642–51), which Hobbes himself experienced, or imagine living in one of the 'failed states' of our times: countries torn apart by horrendous violence and decades of civil war, lacking functioning governments, police or courts to settle disputes, with no infrastructure and a constant lack of food, water, fuel and medicine.

In such a situation, Hobbes claims, people would be motivated solely by self-preservation. They would steal, rob and kill if that was what it took to survive. They would not cultivate land or develop industry because they would know that, as soon as the harvest was ready or the mill built, someone would come and take it. To engage in any long-term or communal project, we need to be able to trust others and make contracts and promises. In a state of nature there is no valid reason why anyone should keep their word because 'the bonds of words are too weak to brindle men's ambition, avarice, anger, and other passions' (p. 100). Hobbes believes, moreover, that in a state of nature people have a natural right to do what it takes to preserve their lives because, in a war of every man against every man, 'nothing can be unjust' (p. 93).

Hobbes's political solution is uncompromising: in such a situation a rational person would choose security over freedom. She would agree to curb her natural egoism and renounce her freedom to do what she wants in order to submit to a political authority with unlimited power. In return, this absolute ruler would keep her safe, enforce rules and punish those who break them. Hobbes calls this absolute ruler *Leviathan* after the powerful monster described in the biblical book of Job.

Hobbes thus reasoned that, because all people, universally, are motivated by self-preservation, they would value their lives and personal safety much more than political freedom. For him, it was evident that chaos, constant fear and violence were far worse than complete obedience, and only someone who had completely lost all reason would prefer such terrors. In other words, people's complete submission to an absolute authority is not a form of slavery, but the most rational choice people can voluntarily make. Hobbes advocates absolute monarchy, not on religious grounds, but on purely rational grounds.

Hobbes's conclusion surely strikes the modern reader as extreme, if not completely crazy. Some readers probably already disagree with his first premise concerning human nature. Feminist political theorists, for example, have raised the question of why people would ever raise children if they were egoists concerned merely with their own survival. They have noted that Hobbes must assume that in a state of nature people procreated by springing up from the ground fully formed like mushrooms. But even readers who are persuaded by his claim that people are natural egoists would surely question whether absolute monarchy provides the only possible solution to conflicts and serves as the sole guarantee of peace.

▶ Locke and the foundations of modern politics

Before the social contract could become the definition of our modern political condition, it thus needed some reworking. We must turn to John Locke (1632–1704), Hobbes's young contemporary, to find the version of the contract – the concepts, ideas and arguments – that we still use today to understand and reflect on contemporary politics. It is Locke who is celebrated as well as criticized for laying the foundations of our Western contemporary liberal and capitalist political order.

Locke powerfully challenged Hobbes's absolutism in *Two Treatises of Government* (1698) and with its publication he became a superstar in the intellectual circles of his time. He shares with Hobbes the idea that the only legitimate basis of power is the consent of the people, and he, too, imagines a state of nature in order to justify the existence of government. But, crucially, he denies that people would ever rationally consent to surrender all power to an absolute sovereign. 'This is to think, that men are so foolish, that they take care to avoid what mischief may be done to them by polecats, or foxes; but are content, nay, think it safety, to be devoured by lions' (Locke, *Two Treatises of Government*, p. 328). In other words, Locke asks why people so concerned about the ferocity of their fellow citizens – polecats and foxes – would submit to the even greater ferocity of sovereigns – lions.

Locke defends the revolutionary idea that people have certain natural and inalienable rights such as the right to life and the right to liberty. We can think of these rights as similar to what we consider human rights today: these natural rights are inalienable in the sense that, regardless of what kind of political or legal system people live in, these rights have to be recognized. Locke's state of nature – the state prior to the social contract and the establishment of government – is thus not a pre-political state of war. It is a state of self-government in which people already have natural rights corresponding to 'the natural law' provided by God and discoverable by reason. This law maintains that all men are free and equal and that they should be treated thus. In other words, for Locke, an objective moral law exists even when there are no policemen or judges to enforce it. In the state of nature, people are entitled not only to defend themselves, but also collectively to pass judgements, impose sanctions and punish natural lawbreakers.

The reason why people agree to form a social contract and establish an institutionalized government is thus not their inability to rule themselves or to live together in peace. Locke argues that, as societies grew larger and more complex, institutionalized political authority proved to be a more effective way of settling disputes and maintaining order. People recognized that it made sense to give up their natural and direct self-government in favour of representative governing institutions. Political power nevertheless fundamentally belongs to the people, which means that if the appointed rulers abuse their power, then the political authority devolves back to the people. Locke argues that in such a situation, the tyrannical ruler effectively puts himself in a state of war against his people by becoming a natural lawbreaker and that the people have the same right to punish him as they would any other lawbreaker in a state of nature. They also have the right to form a new contract and elect a new government.

It is easy to imagine how radical this argument must have been; it effectively legitimizes revolution in certain situations. It proved extremely important for the American Revolution in 1776. The United States Declaration of Independence written by Thomas Jefferson closely follows Locke's *Two Treatises* in its insistence that government must have the consent of the governed and that it is legitimate to overthrow a government when this consent is lacking. In the Declaration's most famous lines, Jefferson also reiterates the idea of the equality of all men as well as the belief in their inalienable, natural and God-given rights: 'We hold these Truths to be self-evident, that all Men are created equal, that they are endowed by their Creator with certain inalienable Rights, that among these are Life, Liberty and the Pursuit of Happiness.'

▶ In defence of private property

Locke also introduced another powerful idea that was to become crucial for the political future of the United States, but one that has proved to be much more controversial. Among the natural rights belonging to all people, not only are there rights to life and liberty, but also the right to own private property. For Hobbes, it made no sense to talk about private property in the state of nature. Nothing could belong to anybody, or everything belonged to everybody until people set up a sovereign power strong enough to establish and protect private property. This meant that people could only have the right to the property granted to them by the sovereign. But, for Locke, one of the inalienable, God-given rights was the right to property, and the principal reason people consented to institutionalized government was their desire to protect this right. Locke's argument about private property remains one of its most influential philosophical defences.

The seventeenth century was an era of dramatic religious and political upheaval in Europe, but it was also the time of rapid and extensive settlement in North America – one of the formative events of the modern world. Locke was directly involved in governing this activity, and the state of nature was therefore no mere thought experiment for him. He imagines the state of nature as a limitless, God-given wilderness: 'in the beginning all the World was America' (p. 301). In discussing the question of property in Chapter 5 of his *Two Treatises*, Locke thus contributed to a bitter dispute over land rights in the American colonies.

Locke argues that God had given the earth to men in general for their enjoyment, but this did not mean that men should leave the earth 'common and uncultivated'. For this reason God gave the earth to 'the industrious and rational'. The fair principle of its distribution is therefore determined by individual labour: earth's resources become private property when someone contributes his labour. Locke reasons that a person naturally owns his body, and therefore, he naturally owns that with which he mixes his labour. His examples include gathering fallen acorns or hunting wild animals: in such cases it seems fair that whoever does the work gets to eat the food, and the acorns and the meat become the labourer's property.

However, Locke also extends the argument to include land. By working the land, workers make the land their property: 'As much land as a man tills, plants, improves, cultivates and can use the product of, so much is his property' (p. 290). Locke qualifies his argument by noting that, in appropriating common resources, a person has to make sure that others are left with 'enough and as good' (p. 288). But he does not explain what happens to those generations of people, no matter how industrious and rational, who arrive on the scene when the land and other limited resources have run out. We might also want to ask him what political principle justifies passing the appropriated land to one's children who might not have done a day's work on it in their lives.

Locke and the appropriation of Native lands

In the context of the European colonization of North America, the political consequences of Locke's argument were momentous. As the political philosopher James Tully (in *An Approach to Political Philosophy*, pp. 137–76) shows, Locke's doctrine effectively made the people who had lived on the land for over 12,000 years – the indigenous peoples – completely insignificant: the land was not their property because they had not mixed their labour with it by cultivating it. The Native Americans did, of course, 'use' the land – they hunted and gathered – but this was not considered 'industrious and rational' use by the Europeans. The European view was that the indigenous peoples possessed only the land they cultivated, and the rest was open for appropriation without their consent; it was nothing but a wasteland of no value, because it had not been improved by commercial agriculture. The European system of individual, labour-based property was thus violently imposed on the indigenous peoples' traditional way of life in which private land ownership made no sense.

In sum, we live in a world fundamentally shaped by Locke's ideas. When we argue that all people should be treated equally or when we criticize authoritarian governments for their human rights abuses, we appeal to his political principles. We also continue to appropriate his views on property. Locke's theory of property justified the English settlement of America and the dispossession of the American Indian First Nations of their property. The violent destruction of indigenous peoples' social and political organizations and the colonial imposition of commercial agriculture were legitimized as a progressive move away from a state of nature to an appropriately political and civilized way of life. The idea that nature can be owned privately and that it has no value unless it produces something economically quantifiable continues to characterize our understanding of it.

5

A just society

ALL THAT MATTERS

'The first person who, having enclosed a plot of land, took it into his head to say this is mine and found people simple enough to believe him, was the true founder of civil society. What crimes, wars, murders, what miseries and horrors would the human race have been spared, had someone pulled up the stakes or filled in the ditch and cried out to his fellow men: 'Do not listen to this impostor. You are lost if you forget that the fruits of the earth belong to all and the earth to no one!'

Rousseau, *Discourse on the Origin of Inequality*, p. 44

Jean-Jacques Rousseau (1712–78) is the last of the great proponents of the social contract, and he transforms it significantly. In his hands it serves two important theoretical functions: it becomes a way of exposing the detestable origins of inequality, war and slavery, and it also becomes the basis for a full-fledged theory of justice. Both of these functions continue in different ways in contemporary political philosophy. Rousseau is the father of those strands of political philosophy aimed at radical social critique as well as those that attempt to formulate standards for an ideally just society.

Rousseau's famous essay *Discourse on the Origin and the Foundations of Inequality among Men* (1755) was written as an entry for the Academy of Dijon's essay contest. A vital issue at the time, which the academy proposed as the essay topic, was: What is the origin of inequality among men, and is it authorized by natural law? In other words, the idea of a natural hierarchy of human beings was still understood to be relevant and worthy of debate. Like other social contract theorists, Rousseau voices a powerful defence of inborn equality against the distorting effects of upbringing, social status and prestige. However, he ridicules Hobbes's state of nature, a war of all against all, as another ridiculous notion of philosophers who make universal claims about human nature 'without leaving their street'. Hobbes's mistake was to take men in the society he knew, transport them in imagination to a state of nature and then make assumptions about human nature on the basis of the premise that men are the same everywhere. For Rousseau, this is like taking a poodle into the forest, observing its behaviour and then drawing inferences about wolves. Rousseau demands that we study actual 'savages' if we want to make claims about a state of nature.

▶ 'Strong, happy, healthy and free'

Rousseau contends that, far from being ferocious egoists, men in their natural condition, lacking all reasons for war, would live in peace. He admits that men are motivated by self-preservation, but their natural appetites are few and easy to satisfy. Moreover, their innate egoism is complemented and limited by an innate compassion for other sentient beings: people will deliberately avoid causing others unnecessary pain and suffering. Rousseau's proofs for the innate goodness of man are interesting because they are based on empirical observations of animals. He discusses the reports on the behaviour of orang-utans by early travellers to the East Indies, for example, and mentions the repugnance of horses for trampling a living body with their hooves. He also puts forward the argument that, because humans have tears, this demonstrates their inborn capacity for compassion.

To be sure, Rousseau's understanding of human nature is optimistic and his view of primitive man – the noble savage – is famously romantic. Man in a state of nature is always healthy and robust, never afraid of danger and totally uncorrupted by vanity, superfluous desires, envy and greed. 'We should not be surprised that the Hottentots of the Cape of Good Hope can sight ships with the naked eye [...] or that these barbarous nations endure their nakedness with no discomfort, whet their appetites with hot peppers, and drink European liquors like water' (p. 24). Whereas man in a state of nature is strong, happy, healthy and free, civilization becomes the source of man's corruption.

Rousseau is well aware that the story he tells about the emergence of inequality cannot be an actual historical account. It is clearly a fictive history, but he intends it to be a philosophically rational account. He

A just society

finds himself living in society in which the laws and social customs clearly produce and protect social inequality. He attempts to trace the logical steps or necessary conditions that could explain this situation and, as we saw in the extract that opens this chapter, he claims that the first step is the idea of the private ownership of property.

With private property men's natural equality is destroyed, and an artificial inequality based on wealth is introduced. As property ownership grows, social problems multiply. With the introduction of agriculture and mining, huge labour resources become necessary. Servitude and domination emerge as men try to increase their wealth by using other men's labour to do so. This introduces conflict and competition. Civilization becomes synonymous with large-scale wars. Public esteem acquires value, and then come vanity and contempt, shame and envy. The last step in Rousseau's account is the exposure of the social contract as a device invented by the most powerful to secure wealth and privilege. The contract, he contends, was an ingenious instrument for legitimizing and protecting existing inequalities and for destroying man's natural liberty. Laws, morals, virtues and philosophical reasoning masked the law of the strongest and took the place of natural compassion. The weak and the poor 'ran to chain themselves, in the belief that they secured their liberty' (p. 56).

Contrary to popular misconception, Rousseau did not suggest that we throw off our clothes, run off to the woods and return to an idyllic state of nature. He believed that, if we could only form the right kind of contract, one that preserved the natural liberty and equality of men, then the advantages of entering organized society would far outweigh the simple pleasures possible in a state of nature. In society, men can engage in intellectual and artistic pursuits, as well as follow genuine moral principles and rules of reason to order their impulses. Most importantly, justice is possible only in an organized society. In a state of nature the notion of justice is meaningless, and debating it, senseless.

In his most famous work, *The Social Contract* (1762), Rousseau outlines an ideal contract that preserves the freedom and equality of all citizens. People must freely constitute a political collective, and each of its members must have equal political authority regardless of birth or wealth. The members must publicly deliberate on the laws and principles that govern their way of living. For Rousseau, the only legitimate political authority – sovereignty – is *popular sovereignty*: citizens governing themselves. The power of the people is inalienable, meaning that it cannot be transferred to a separate authority or sovereign and the people cannot be represented by anyone else. The people can obviously elect governors and deputies for themselves, but the role of such governors is solely to minister the will of the people. The elected cannot rule the people or make decisions for them. In entering into a social contract, people must freely form a political collective. This means that they never hand over their natural liberty to anyone else – except to themselves as a collective; therefore, after forming the contract, they 'remain as free as before'.

DU

CONTRACT SOCIAL;

O U,

PRINCIPES

D U

DROIT POLITIQUE.

PAR J. J. ROUSSEAU,
CITOYEN DE GENEVE.

Dicamus leges, — *fœderis æquas*
Æneid. XI.

A AMSTERDAM,
Chez MARC MICHEL REY.
MDCCLXII.

▲ First published in 1762, Jean-Jacques Rousseau's *Du contrat social* [The Social Contract] – with its radical ideas about 'people power' – helped inspire the French Revolution of 1789.

While Hobbes had likewise held that the people were the final source of political authority, he had argued that in entering the social contract they gave up their sovereignty by transferring all power to an absolute ruler. Locke, too, had insisted that the government depended on the people's consent, but for him the consent of the people was something essentially tacit and assumed. Its only real expression was the extreme event of a revolution. Rousseau's idea of popular sovereignty is a much more radical idea of self-government because he insists that the consent of the people has to have a real means of expression. He argues for the importance of people's assemblies in which the people publicly deliberate on fundamental political issues and in which their active agreement – *the general will* – can be regularly voiced and renewed.

The general will is Rousseau's most famous, but also his most controversial, idea. For him, popular sovereignty, the legitimacy of government and ultimately the existence of the state must be founded on the general will – the common will of all the people acting together. It is easy to make the mistake of thinking that the general will means the same thing as the will of the majority, because this is how we mostly understand democratic decision-making in parliaments today. Votes express preferences, and voting provides the best available mechanism for reconciling the different interests of a people. Hence, if we submit a proposal to a vote in a people's assembly, the will of the majority becomes the common will of the people.

Rousseau, however, makes it clear that the general will is not the will of the majority. It is not some kind of aggregate of individual wills, but a qualitatively different kind of will. He acknowledges that individuals have particular wills determined by self-interest: members of a community do not always will the same thing, but have many conflicting interests and goals. However, as citizens, their decisions cannot be guided by narrow self-interest. So, in addition to their individual, private will, people have a will as citizens to which the general will corresponds. In other words, citizens have to be able to reach decisions that are best for the whole community, and this means accepting that the common good may sometimes be in conflict with their partisan, personal interests. It is not difficult to imagine examples: as an individual, I would like to park my car in front of my office in the historic town centre, but, as a citizen concerned about pollution and the vitality of my city, I strongly support a traffic ban in that area. Obeying the general will thus does not mean submitting to someone else's authority, since the general will is in fact my own will as a rational citizen. Obeying it means obeying only myself.

Rousseau's thought thus brings about a radical shift in perspective: politics is not a realm in which everyone tries to advance his or her own preferences and interests. It is not about asking what is good for *me*; I must ask what is good for *us*. Rousseau believes that a contentious understanding of politics can be overcome by refocusing political decision-making and debate on the ideas of justice and the common good.

▶ Rawls and justice

Rousseau's attempt to formulate an ideal contract was continued in twentieth-century political philosophy by John Rawls (1921–2002) in his highly influential *Theory of Justice* (1971). Similar to Rousseau, Rawls sets out to identify the principles regulating an ideally just society. His book famously begins with the claim that justice is the most important virtue of social institutions, just as truth is the most important virtue of scientific theories. 'A theory however elegant and economical must be rejected or revised if it is untrue; likewise laws and institutions, no matter how efficient and well-arranged, must be reformed or abolished if they are unjust.' (Rawls, *Theory of Justice*, p. 3).

Like Rousseau, Rawls contends that the principles of justice have to be established by a decision-making procedure involving all the members to whom the principles are to apply. However, Rawls does not imagine this procedure as a regularly convened public assembly in which the citizens of an actual community make decisions about the laws under which they live. Rather, he formulates the process as a purely imaginary meeting. His version of the social contract is thus more like a Hobbesian thought experiment, which emphasizes rational choice. Instead of a state of nature, Rawls imagines 'an original position of equality', a hypothetical situation in which people freely select, once and for all, the principles of justice regulating their society and its allocation of goods, liberties and opportunities.

The 'veil of ignorance'

In Rawls's thought experiment, people must make this selection behind a 'veil of ignorance'. This means that they must select these principles not knowing what their own situation would be in that society: they are ignorant of their class position and social status, as well as of their natural assets and abilities such as intelligence, strength and other talents. In other words, the veil of ignorance functions as a test of fairness, similar to trying to make sure that a cake is fairly divided by deciding that the person who cuts it must not know which piece he or she is going to get. The veil of ignorance ensures that everyone is similarly situated and unable to design or select principles that would favour his or her particular situation.

If we were to follow Rawls's thought experiment, what principles would we choose? Rawls argues that if people choose rationally – and he assumes that they always do – then they will inevitably select the principles that maximize what they get if they end up in the worst-off position in their society. Even if people do not know what social position they will occupy, there are things they know for certain they will want and need in order to have a good life. Some of these things are distributed by social institutions, and Rawls calls them 'social primary goods'. These goods include liberties, rights and opportunities, income and wealth, as well as the basis of self-respect. Rawls argues that people will always attempt to maximize their share of these goods, and this means that they will favour a distribution that maximizes the smallest share.

Rawls emphasizes that his course of action does not imply that people are natural egoists. Since no one knows his position in society, asking individuals to decide what is best for themselves has the same consequence as asking them to put themselves in everyone else's shoes and impartially decide what is best for them. However, the advantage of Rawls's method is that the principles the individual chooses are not only fair according to some abstract principle of benevolence, but also the result of rational choice.

Rawls claims that the principles chosen in this hypothetical thought experiment also correspond to our intuitively held views of justice as equality. Attempting to maximize what one gets if one ended up in the worst position in society translates into the principle that social goods should be divided equally, with one important caveat: 'unless an unequal distribution of any or all of these goods is to the advantage of the least favored' (p. 303). In other words, Rawls claims that the principle of equality does not require that we simply remove all inequalities. Unequal distribution is fair if it compensates for some disadvantage, for example. Some inequalities also benefit everyone by promoting useful talents and ambitions. If we give a medical researcher a large grant and with the help of it she discovers a cure for cancer, this unequal distribution of money not only benefits her personally but, more importantly, is also to the advantage of cancer patients. Rawls contends that, as long an unequal distribution of resources, liberties or opportunities can be shown to ameliorate the situation of the worst-off people, it accords with our sense of justice.

Rawls's theory is thus strongly egalitarian, emphasizing equal opportunities, resources and liberties, and he defends redistributive measures as a way of levelling social inequalities and ensuring social justice. Many see his theory as a theoretical defence of the post-war capitalist welfare state, which mixes market freedoms with state services and progressive taxation. In political philosophy Rawls's ideas have set the tone for debate in Anglo-American normative political theory in the last 40 years in a way that is unparalleled. Contemporary utilitarianism, libertarianism and communitarianism have developed as identifiable schools of political philosophy largely as critical responses to different aspects of Rawls's theory. We will look at some of their key ideas in the chapters that follow. We also need to discuss the central ideas of Rawls's more radical critics, the Marxists and feminists, who have claimed that his redistributive principles do not go nearly far enough towards establishing equality: redistribution will not challenge the entrenched power relations that involve class, race and gender.

6

The power of reason

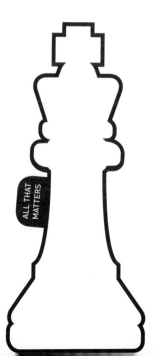

'*Enlightenment is man's emergence from his self-incurred immaturity. Immaturity is the inability to use one's own understanding without the guidance of another. This immaturity is self-incurred if its cause is not lack of understanding, but lack of resolution and courage to use it without the guidance of another. The motto of enlightenment is therefore:* Sapere aude! *Have the courage to use your own understanding!*'

Kant, *Political Writings*, p. 54

It is difficult to imagine a political upheaval today that would parallel the significance of the American and French Revolutions at the end of the eighteenth century. Not only did these revolutions fundamentally transform the political geography of Europe and North America; they also annihilated the taken-for-granted certitudes in political thought. Traditional political principles and the deeply rooted hierarchies based on them – monarchy, aristocracy and religious authority – were abruptly overthrown and replaced by the new ideals of liberty, equality and fraternity.

Although the American and French Revolutions were unprecedented events, they did not take place in a cultural and intellectual vacuum. The radical ideas of Locke and Rousseau discussed in the previous chapters clearly sustained them – the freedom and equality of the people as well as their natural right to govern themselves. These revolutions were also inseparable from a series of social, political and intellectual transformations usually referred to as the Enlightenment – an intellectual and cultural movement that dominated eighteenth-century thought.

The Enlightenment is also called the Age of Reason because its basic idea was that only the critical use of reason should direct society and politics. In the same way that truths in science could be discovered, demonstrated and agreed upon by all rational thinkers, so a rational and just political order could similarly be established. Prejudices and fears, disagreements and conflicts, illusions and myths were all consequences of ignorance and irrationality, and these could be dissipated by the light of reason.

▶ Kant and the rule of reason

The philosophical ideas that define the Enlightenment converge in the political writings of Immanuel Kant (1724–1804). His thought articulates in clear terms its central convictions: universal laws governing morality, politics and history could be established and investigated by rational minds, and consequently the increase of rational knowledge would inevitably lead to progress. He believed that, just as scientific knowledge in his time had resulted in enormous progress in medicine and agriculture, such progress in political matters was possible, too. The Enlightenment presented an unequalled opportunity, as well as making a moral claim on us to use our reason critically and publicly for the good of humanity.

Kant was a strong defender of the rule of law as the ultimate guarantee, not only of security and peace, but also of freedom. He believed that human societies were moving towards more rational forms regulated by effective and binding legal frameworks because only such frameworks enabled people to live in harmony, to prosper and to co-operate. However, his belief in inevitable progress was not based on an optimistic or high-minded view of human nature. On the contrary, it comes close to Hobbes's outlook: man's violent and conflict-prone nature makes it necessary to establish and maintain an effective legal framework in order to secure peace. We cannot count on people's benevolence or goodwill, but even 'a nation of devils' can live in harmony in a legal system that binds every citizen equally (p. 112). Ideally, the law is the embodiment of those political principles that all rational beings would freely choose. If such laws forbid them to do something that they would not rationally choose to do anyway, then the law cannot be understood as a restraint on their freedom. Being law-abiding, obeying one's own rational mind and being wholly free amount to the same thing.

Kant also deeply believes that legality can only triumph if the rule of law prevails in all states, not just some, as well as in the international relations between states.

If a particular state should manage to erect and maintain an effective legal system, its citizens would not be able to enjoy fully the security guaranteed by the law unless they were also able to avoid conflicts with other states. Universal justice and security are ultimately possible only if war can be abolished as a tool of politics, and peace established and safeguarded according to global principles of what is right. Kant thus, importantly, developed the social contract theory into an international and cosmopolitan idea.

While a world government administering universal law would be the most effective way to end war, Kant acknowledged that the achievement of such political order would be highly unrealistic. States are not likely to agree to surrender their sovereignty completely, nor is the territory of the world compact enough to make it possible to govern centrally. Instead, Kant advocates a voluntary federation of states opposed to war. He sees such an outcome as inevitable because it is the only rational solution to the central problem of politics – how to guarantee the peace and security that make prosperity, productivity and progress possible. He believes that nations, like individuals, will eventually come to the rational conclusion that it is more beneficial to agree to international law as a means of settling disputes than to engage in costly and destructive wars. The respect for domestic law in individual states will thus expand to an international system of laws. 'The peoples of the earth have thus entered in varying degrees into a universal community, and it has developed to the point where a violation of the rights in *one* part of the world is felt *everywhere*' (pp. 107–8).

Kant was ahead of his time in recognizing that only a few political problems can be confined strictly within the borders of individual nation-states. One of the main challenges of political philosophers today is to continue Kant's project by responding adequately to globalization and inquiring into the possibility of a just global political order. Kant's idea of a federation of states opposed to war can also be understood to correspond to the League of Nations after the First World War and to the current United Nations.

Yet Kant seems to have also been profoundly mistaken: his optimistic views about humanity's inevitable progress towards perpetual peace have been contradicted by the horrendous wars of modern Western life. In a world in which wars are often fought in faraway countries and arms are sold and shipped across oceans, there are perfectly rational, economic incentives for states to promote war rather than peace. Moreover, a more profound critique of the Enlightenment would claim that it is precisely the Enlightenment principles themselves that have led to war rather than to peace.

▶ Critiquing the Enlightenment

Dialectic of Enlightenment (1944), a book by the Frankfurt School philosophers Theodor W. Adorno (1903–69) and Max Horkheimer (1895–1973), is arguably the most influential critical assessment of the Enlightenment. The book was written in California in the aftermath of the Second World

War during the writers' exile from Nazi Germany. Adorno and Horkheimer here articulate, in powerful terms, the painful loss of faith in the political potential of reason. The nineteenth century had already been marked by expansive wars and brutal colonialist violence, but in the twentieth century the Holocaust became a symbol of horror unrivalled in history: it took the cold rationality of effective killing to a new level. Rather than leading to perpetual peace, the Enlightenment had culminated in the most extensive and technologically sophisticated violence ever seen. Despite all of civilization's scientific knowledge and rational capacities, millions of people had ended up supporting an utterly irrational fascist ideology. They had used their sophisticated understanding of science and technology to organize genocide and launch atom bombs, not to eradicate poverty or disease.

▲ The extermination camps built by Nazi Germany during the Second World War used 'rationality' and 'science' to carry out the murders of millions of people, and as such have been seen as on the dead ends of the 'Enlightenment project'.

Adorno and Horkheimer see fascism in their native Germany as well as the consumer capitalism and 'candy-floss entertainment' of California as different manifestations of the Enlightenment project. When reason is elevated as the sole, highest principle organizing politics, we end up with new and devastating forms of domination: political systems that are maximally effective and functional, but empty of meaning and capable of the most horrendous atrocities.

It is important to note that Adorno and Horkheimer do not simply place the blame on science or scientists, but engage in a more profound and searching critique of modern rationality. The advancement of reason made it possible to explain and control both nature and society, but at the same time this control became a new form of domination. Enlightenment reason was essentially *instrumental reason*: it was a tool of domination empty of any substantive goals or meanings. Adorno and Horkheimer attempt to expose the false reasoning of Enlightenment thinkers such as Kant, who saw reason as inevitably leading to moral progress. Formalistic, instrumental reason was no more closely allied to morality than to immorality. They argue provocatively that the Marquis de Sade – the notorious father of sadism – should be revered as the true philosopher of the Enlightenment because of the honesty with which he mercilessly demonstrated the consequences of Enlightenment thought for morality. He 'trumpeted far and wide the impossibility of deriving from reason any fundamental argument against murder' (Horkheimer and Adorno, *Dialectic of Enlightenment*, p. 118).

The secularization that characterized the Enlightenment thus raises a serious philosophical problem. Religion was capable of grounding morality as well as providing substantial political goals – it seemed to provide strong motivation and a desire to be good and to develop societies that were fair. When religion was replaced by instrumental reason, we all became either Machiavellian or hypocritical because it was equally rational, or sometimes even more rational, to act in ways that were unjust. Reason 'permits peace or war, tolerance or repression' (p. 87). Since it posits no substantial goals, it can be attached to any political ends.

Dialectic of Enlightenment also engages in a performative contradiction, however: it seems to do the opposite of what it says. A critique of society, such as Horkheimer and Adorno present, can only be conducted by means of rational argument. While putting forward a critique of reason, their own project nevertheless relies on reason's ability to scrutinize itself critically and to formulate rational arguments about the current problems in society and politics. Despite their radical critique of the Enlightenment project, Adorno and Horkheimer cannot, and do not, totally abandon its ideals.

▶ Thinking for oneself

In addition to the belief in universal laws and inevitable progress that I have highlighted here, the Enlightenment faith in reason translates into a critical attitude. As the famous extract opening this chapter states, the motto of the Enlightenment according to Kant is *sapere audi*: have the courage to think for yourself. Significantly, the critical attitude that we have inherited from the Enlightenment means that we cannot blindly trust political authorities and experts, nor can we swallow dogmatic beliefs uncritically. We must have the courage to use our own reason and understanding also in political matters.

Many political thinkers today see this demand for critical thought, argumentation and debate as the most important legacy of the Enlightenment: we must counter the authority of tradition with the force of a better argument. Jürgen Habermas (born 1929), a student of Adorno and today one of the most influential political philosophers in the world, continues the Enlightenment project in just such a critical form. His constant concern has been to safeguard the possibility of rational, democratic deliberation in secular modern societies in which shared and authoritative religious norms have dissolved. For Habermas, such rational discussion is fundamental to politics: the only legitimate way for people to organize their lives communally and to decide what common rules they want to live by is through public deliberation – processes of political argumentation and rational justification.

Instead of instrumental rationality – the type of rationality so lamented by Adorno and Horkheimer – Habermas emphasizes *communicative rationality*, which makes critical discussion and mutual understanding possible. For him, reason is primarily a feature of human communication in so far as communication is oriented towards understanding one another and engagement in communication is always implicitly a commitment to explaining and justifying our views with reasons. Habermas also believes that it could be possible to reach a genuine consensus on a range of political matters through an unconstrained, rational dialogue, as long as all speakers had equal access to the discussion and only the force of the better argument prevailed. In other words, the participants in such political deliberation must presuppose that anyone affected by the issues under consideration can take part in the discussion and that each participant is free to introduce and challenge arguments. The participants must also treat each other as equals, reciprocally acknowledging one another's right to voice their views.

Habermas's key claim is that the ideals he identifies as regulating political deliberation – equality, reciprocity, inclusion and generalizability – are not abstract moral principles imposed on the participants from some philosophically privileged standpoint. Rather, they are pragmatically, and often tacitly, presupposed by the participants themselves. People must presuppose these principles in the sense that, without so doing, they would not be able to claim that a political argument was truly justified. If someone with important things to say about an issue were to be excluded from the discussion, or if the person had been coerced into agreeing to the claims being made, the decision could not be understood as the outcome of fair political deliberation.

This does not mean that the presuppositions of ideal communication could ever be fully realized in actual deliberation. In reality, deliberative practices can always be developed, and communication across social differences and power imbalances improved. For

Habermas, identifying and analysing such idealized presuppositions is crucial because it provides grounds for criticizing those political practices that do not meet their own implicit presuppositions. Following Kant and other Enlightenment thinkers, he advocates an open society in which politics must be essentially shaped by criticism and the processes of free and rational public discussion.

'Postmodern' political thought

In contemporary political philosophy, Habermas and other political thinkers who are continuing the Enlightenment project are often placed in opposition to those critics called 'postmodern' – philosophers such as Michel Foucault, Jacques Derrida and contemporary political thinkers influenced by their ideas. This label is not only confusing and vague but also misleading, because it suggests that these thinkers advocate a complete break with the Enlightenment. Instead of attempting to move beyond it in some way, they have raised critical questions about the Enlightenment's universalist political assumptions. Are the ideals and principles of reason truly universal in the sense that they are discoverable by all rational thinkers, instead of being historically and culturally contingent, specifically Western ideals? How can we be sure that all rational beings would freely choose these principles, given ideal circumstances? Could it be that Europe just happened to invent such ideals as 'individual freedom' and 'human rights' and then managed to elevate these local ideas to universal political principles? Is the contemporary Western worldview, characterized by scientific rationality and atomistic individuality, really the most progressive way of relating to the world and to others?

In sum, the legacy of the Enlightenment is, and must continue to be, divided and heterogeneous. It is no exaggeration to say that this legacy frames many of our most pressing political problems, challenges and debates today, ranging from the contested meaning of 9/11 and the role of religion in politics to the possibility of global democracy. A key issue in these debates continues to be the contested role of universal reason in politics.

7

Liberty

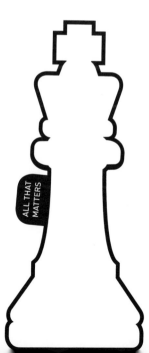

'The object of this essay is to assert one very simple principle, as entitled to govern absolutely the dealings of society with the individual in the way of compulsion and control, whether the means used be physical force in the form of legal penalties or the moral coercion of public opinion. That principle is that the sole end for which mankind are warranted, individually or collectively, in interfering with the liberty of action of their number is self-protection. That the only purpose for which power can be rightfully exercised over any member of a civilized community, against his will, is to prevent harm to others. His own good, either physical or moral, is not a sufficient warrant.'

Mill, *On Liberty*, p. 68

To read John Stuart Mill's *On Liberty* (1859) today, more than 150 years after its publication, might feel like going over ideas that have become so thoroughly familiar as to be almost self-evident. His short but extremely influential book is an impassioned defence of many of the ideas and values that we consider definitive of our modern, Western way of life: the importance of free speech, cultural diversity and religious tolerance for the intellectual and political life of a community, and the value of originality, creativity and spontaneity for the wellbeing and full development of the individual. Yet Mill's basic principle, expressed in the extract above, namely that a liberal government is not entitled to interfere in the private life of the individual unless that individual is causing real harm to others, continues to be strongly opposed in many parts of the world. For example, for most of us, the idea that homosexuality should be legally punishable at all is abhorrent, never mind punishable by life imprisonment or the death penalty; yet this is the reality in many countries today.

As I have shown in the previous chapters, the idea that all human beings (men) were born free was a well-established political principle by the nineteenth century, when Mill wrote his book. The idea of liberty was also vehemently argued for by a number of his contemporaries, such as William Godwin, Henry David Thoreau and Pierre-Joseph Proudhon. It was Mill, however, who converted this idea into a comprehensive and systematic political doctrine and gave liberalism the philosophical form in which it is still discussed and debated today.

Utilitarianism

John Stuart Mill was educated at home by his father, James Mill, a well-known champion of utilitarian philosophy and a close associate of Jeremy Bentham (1748–1832), the father of utilitarianism. Utilitarianism continues to be an influential, if contested, strand of moral and political philosophy, and it has undergone several different formulations since Bentham. Its core ideas are that moral actions should be judged solely by their consequences and that the morally right act or policy is that which produces the greatest happiness for the members of a society.

For Bentham, the greatest happiness could be calculated by evaluating individual pleasures and pains, although many later utilitarians have recognized the problems with his crude calculus. They have sought to refine the theory by defining happiness in more sophisticated ways – promoting the maximal satisfaction of people's informed preferences, for example. Influential philosophers such as John Rawls have sharply criticized utilitarianism, however, showing how this philosophy could justify sacrificing the weak and unpopular members of a society for the benefit of the majority. Many contemporary political philosophers have also deemed utilitarianism too narrow a philosophical framework for analysing current political practices: a focus solely on utility excludes considerations of personal responsibility and duty, as well as considerations of the basic rights of individuals.

Although Mill wrote widely on utilitarianism and worked closely with the utilitarians of his time, his *On Liberty* is a departure from purely utilitarian principles. Mill does defend liberty and the sovereignty of the individual on utilitarian grounds; he argues, for example, that the intellectual and cultural progress of a community depends on the originality of some of its members, and it is therefore to the benefit of all that individuals are left to pursue their own interests. But he also defends the intrinsic value of liberty itself. Liberty is thus defended not only as a means to an end – the greatest happiness or wellbeing of the people – but also because it is valuable in itself.

▶ The individual and society

Mill's argument starts with a detailed defence of free thought and discussion. Once its importance is established, Mill follows up with the question of whether the same reasons do not require that people should also be free to act upon their opinions – to engage in different experiments of living and in the cultivation of their individuality, originality and genius. This leads to the political question of the rightful limits of the sovereignty of the individual over himself: how much of human life should be controlled by the individual and how much by society.

As Mill himself summarizes his argument, he is defending two, seemingly simple, maxims. The first is that 'the individual is not accountable to society for his actions in so far as these concern the interests of no person but himself' (p. 163). In other words, the government cannot legally interfere in an individual's actions or way of life, no matter how bizarre, immoral or dangerous, as long as these actions do not harm others in any way. We can try to advise, warn or persuade people to mend their ways – Mill would probably approve of the warnings on packs of cigarettes – and we can avoid the company of derelict individuals. But the state cannot interfere legally or by force as long as the harm caused affects only the person himself. Mill's examples include many liberties that we take for granted today, but that were controversial at the time: a person should be able to get as drunk as she wants as long as she is not performing some public duty; she should be free to follow any variety of religious and cultural conventions, such as not eating pork, and she should be able to express and argue her views freely.

The other maxim states that, for those actions that in any way harm others, or in Mill's words, 'are prejudicial to the interests of others', the individual must be legally accountable. In those situations the government must interfere in order to protect other members of its society.

While these key principles of *On Liberty* seem exceptionally clear, they nevertheless raise difficult questions, which continue to be debated today in liberal democracies. For example, what is considered harmful to others is often a matter of interpretation. It can be argued that almost everything I do has some indirect consequences for other people. Liberalism's core principle, freedom of speech, also continues to cause bitter disagreement. Does this principle mean that we have to tolerate even *hate speech* – speech disparaging a racial, sexual or ethnic group or a member of such a group?

▲ The issue of hate speech continues to test the parameters of liberty in Western democratic states.

Many people who are strongly opposed to racism and sexism follow Mill and argue that we should tolerate such speech. Some argue, on utilitarian grounds, that encouraging free debate is more likely to generate an open-minded, free-thinking society in which racial prejudice is questioned and will eventually disappear. Others base their support of this freedom on the intrinsic value of liberty: people's freedom to think and say even the unthinkable must be safeguarded in liberal democracies. In their view, interfering with the right to freedom of speech ultimately poses a greater risk to a viable democracy than racist language.

Yet Mill's defence of free speech does not warrant hate speech or racial abuse if we keep in mind that his second key principle unequivocally prohibits action that is harmful to others. What the defenders of unlimited freedom of speech often overlook is that hate speech is not just words, but an action that causes real effects in the world. It causes real harm to its targets, ranging from physiological symptoms and emotional distress to restrictions on personal security and freedom. In liberal democracies freedom of expression must be protected, but this cannot be done at an unfair cost to some people. Furthermore, most people would hold that freedom of expression is important because it allows both individuals and societies to flourish. Hate speech has the opposite effect, not only for the victims of racist abuse and so on, but also for the societies that tolerate such abuse.

▶ Economic liberalism

Before moving on to discuss the critiques of liberalism in the next chapter, I must first talk about money. It is often claimed, insistently, that political liberalism only tells half the story: what, in fact, has most profoundly changed our way of life as well as our conception of politics is not the principle of individual liberty but economic liberalism – the principle of free trade. While these two strands of liberalism are intertwined, they rely on different arguments. Mill was a strong supporter of economic liberalism, but he made clear in *On Liberty* that the argument for free trade must rest on different grounds from his defence of the principle of individual liberty.

The most common argument today for free trade and unrestricted markets is their productivity. In many instances, even socialist parties have ended up supporting the abolishment of market restrictions on the grounds that this leads to greater productivity, which in turn leads to greater wealth, making it possible for governments to achieve greater equality and welfare through various redistributive schemes and social services. At the opposite end of the political spectrum, libertarians such as Robert Nozick strongly defend market freedoms, but not (primarily) on account of their productivity, but rather because the free market is inherently just. Libertarians are strongly opposed to the role of the state in implementing social policy and for enforcing redistributive taxation schemes because they see such programmes as violations of the individual's right to private property and of the ability to decide freely how to exercise that right.

Adam Smith's *An Inquiry into the Nature and Causes of the Wealth of Nations* (1776), by far the most influential defence of free trade ever written, can be used to support the idea that free trade leads to greater productivity as well as the idea that free trade is morally just. Even if the book is often celebrated for inaugurating modern economics, its enormous influence is largely owing to its powerful combination of economic insights with political philosophy and social theory. This has made the *Wealth of Nations* (as it is often called) fundamental to a distinct political worldview that links economic freedom with political freedom.

Adam Smith (1723–90) was a key figure in the Scottish Enlightenment. For him, free trade was an essential means of achieving progress and human equality: free trade would eradicate desperate poverty and erode ingrained class hierarchies because free markets mean that everyone can compete on equal terms. In contrast, a system in which a government grants special privileges to certain merchants and producers by imposing trade regulations and barriers or by establishing monopolies is an effective way of protecting special business interests against the interests of the public, who are the consumers.

The 'invisible hand'

Smith makes the famous argument that, if markets were left free of political interference, it would be as though an 'invisible hand' were directing everyone's activities to optimize the outcome for all. The invisible hand thus refers to a spontaneous, unintended causal mechanism that explains social order: it ensures that supply and demand adjust to a natural balance and that the collective result of each person pursuing his or her own individual interest results in the promotion of the collective good – economic prosperity. With witty sarcasm, Smith comments on the behaviour of merchants:

> *'By pursuing his own interest he [the merchant] frequently promotes that of the society more effectually than when he really intends to promote it. I have never known much good done by those who affected to trade for the public good. It is an affectation, indeed, not very common among merchants, and very few words need be employed in dissuading them from it.'*
>
> (Adam Smith, *Wealth of Nations*, p. 351)

Liberty

For Smith, capitalism, or a free market economy, is the natural economic order because it is based on people's natural propensity to 'truck, barter and exchange' and is regulated by the rules of exchange emerging from people's inborn self-regard. This self-regard translates into the spontaneous regulation of prices in a free market because people will buy or sell only when it is beneficial for them to do so and at a price they consider profitable. Smith also assumes that the different economic classes in society – capitalists, landowners and labourers – naturally co-operate because it is to their mutual benefit. If market conditions change so that wages, profits or rents sink too low and this co-operation is no longer beneficial to some, then those individuals will withdraw. We will see in the next chapter how Karl Marx fundamentally challenges this idea of a natural and spontaneous order in capitalism.

Smith's argument for free trade thus combines economic and political ideas: protectionism both hinders economic growth and violates the principle of equal opportunity. Today many people defend capitalism for a third reason as well: they argue that it is the only economic system compatible with democracy. The popularity of Friedrich Hayek's *The Road to Serfdom* (1944) – arguably one of the most influential books of the twentieth century – was largely owing to his ability to formulate a defence of free-market capitalism in such a form. Hayek's claim is that socialism or any form of a centrally planned or regulated economy inevitably leads to coercion because this is the only way central planning on a large scale is possible. Socialist ideals of economic equality can only be effectively put into practice by a strong, dictatorial government. Planning is always a form of discipline that has to be imposed by force, and a centralized economic power creates a degree of dependency that is scarcely distinguishable from slavery. The more governments control economic matters, the more they are able to control all other aspects of our lives because controlling economic activity means controlling the limited means for all our ends. 'And whoever has control of the means must also determine which ends are to be served, which values are to be rated higher and which lower, in short, what men should believe and strive for' (Hayek, *The Road to Serfdom*, pp. 68–9).

The quickest way to demolish Hayek's argument on the necessary link between capitalism and democracy is simply to assess it on empirical grounds – by observing the world around us. If we study existing political systems, we soon see that democracy and capitalism do not necessarily go hand in hand. At the moment Saudi Arabia and Oman, for example, combine capitalism with absolute monarchy. Capitalism and right-wing dictatorships have also co-existed, for example, in Portugal and Chile in the 1970s. The reverse also seems to be true: in the Nordic countries socialist economic policies have been successfully combined with democratic governance. However, if we want to evaluate capitalism on philosophical grounds, then we will have to dig deeper. So let's give voice to its radical critics and see what they make of capitalism.

8

Marxists and anarchists

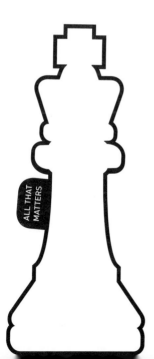

'One thing, however, is clear: nature does not produce on the one hand owners of money or commodities, and on the other hand men possessing nothing but their own labour-power. This relation has no basis in natural history, nor does it have a social basis common to all periods of human history. It is clearly the result of past historical development, the product of many economic revolutions, of the extinction of a whole series of older formations of social production.'

Marx, *Capital*, p. 273

When Marx is included in introductions to political philosophy, the focus is often on his early writings in which he anticipates the twentieth-century *communitarian* critique of liberalism: a political theory that begins with an isolated individual is bound to lead to absurd political consequences. Like Marx, contemporary communitarians, such as Michael Walzer and Michael Sandel, have argued that people are always members of communities, and only their fundamental social bonds and familial ties make individual interests and goals possible. Liberal rights thus falsely equate liberty with protected isolation.

My focus here will be on Marx's most important work, *Capital* (vol. 1, 1867). The work might appear to be a treatise on economic theory rather than a critique of liberalism, but its fundamental aim is deeply political: to reveal how the supposedly scientific and politically neutral economic theories and policies upholding liberal capitalist societies mask highly exploitative power relations. In other words, its goal is to free us from ideology – a system of beliefs that reflects a false perception of reality distorted by interests of the dominant class. The key liberalist idea of a 'free market' was, according to Marx, one such ideology.

▶ Exposing the logic of capitalism

Enlightenment thinkers and liberal economists such as Adam Smith had argued that free trade and industrialization would inevitably bring about prosperity and improve the lives of common people. If a machine could do in an hour what a man could do in a day, then it seemed inevitable that such increased productivity would necessarily result in more free time and more affordable goods. Observing the lives of the working classes in Britain, the country that was leading industrialization in his time, Marx realized that neither outcome had come about. Instead, Britain's industrial cities were awash with human beings living in abject poverty. Working conditions in the new factories were extremely harsh and dangerous, children formed an integral part of the workforce, and labour laws and regulations were either non-existent or highly exploitative. While some people were growing richer, others had become so poor that their lives could barely be called human.

Marx wanted to expose the fundamental mechanisms that govern the capitalist mode of production in order to explain such a situation. He needed to explain why, in a capitalist system, improved productivity due to industrialization did not automatically lead to a shorter workday or to better wages for the workers, for example. The small improvements in the workers' situations – the legal limitations on the length of the working day to twelve hours for miners and eight hours for children or legislation that put the minimum age for child labourers at nine, for example – resulted from hard political struggle, not from the advances of free trade.

For Marx, an obvious problem with the idyllic picture that Adam Smith purveys of the 'free market' was that the worker and the capitalist were not in a symmetrical situation when they came to exchange their products – labour power for money. The capitalist was not forced to buy anything because he was in a position to wait, move his factory elsewhere, or reinvest his money in something else. The worker, on the other hand, could not wait. He constantly had to sell his labour power if he wanted to survive, because in a capitalist system all

▲ Marx analysed the ruthless mechanisms that lay behind capitalism, exposing, for example, the links between child labour and the products consumed by the wealthier members of society.

other means of making a living had been eradicated. Marx argues that a society of landless wage-labourers with nothing but their labour power to sell was an historical outcome of the social upheaval that followed the breakdown of feudalism. It was not a result of some natural inequality of talents and preferences – some people did not freely choose to become workers and some capitalists. Deliberate and violent political acts, such as the appropriation of common resources and property legislation favouring rich landowners, led to the accumulation of property and raw materials into the hands of a few and made it necessary for the vast masses of landless peasants to sell their labour power.

In other words, in the new commercial society organized on the principles of private ownership and monetary exchanges there was an institutionalized compulsion for the worker to sell his labour power.

Surplus value

Apart from the asymmetry in the process of exchange between the worker and the capitalist, Marx argues that there is a more fundamental problem inherent in the capitalist mode of production itself. He attempts to expose the problem with his idea of *surplus value*. For Marx, human labour is an important and curious source of wealth because it is capable of generating more value than is required for its reproduction, or, in other words, for keeping the labourer alive and healthy. Different economic systems have appropriated this truth in different ways. When the medieval serf worked half a week for his own livelihood and the other half without pay on the estate of his lord, the appropriation of the surplus value generated by his labour was immediately visible. The same is true of slavery: the work of slaves was appropriated by their owners without any compensation other than the bare minimum required to sustain them. Marx argues that a similar appropriation of surplus value generated by the unpaid labour of workers is also the source of wealth in the 'free market' of a capitalist economy. However, now the process is disguised so that we do not recognize it immediately.

What essentially defines the capitalist system of production, according to Marx, is that labour power itself has become a commodity, something that can be separated from the worker, from his interests and goals, and bought and sold in the market. The capitalist owns and controls the means of production, such as machinery and raw materials, and, by 'combining' them with the labour power that he buys from the workers, is able to produce commodities with value. He himself does not work, however, and hence does not generate any value, but only appropriates the value generated by other people's work. The longer, or more intensively, the labourers work, the more value their labour generates for him. The capitalist gives back part of that value to the worker as wages so that the worker can reproduce his labour power – eat, sleep and feed his children. Part goes to cover the cost of raw materials and other expenses. The rest, however, the capitalist keeps for himself. This profit is value generated by the workers, too, but it does not benefit them, as it goes to the capitalist alone.

Marx insists that capitalist exploitation does not consist solely of the capitalist keeping the profits for himself. In other words, capitalism would not be 'fair' even if the worker and the capitalist shared the profits equally. The more fundamental problem would still remain, namely that both the wage that the capitalist pays the worker for his labour power and the money with which he buys the raw materials is already value that some other worker, not the capitalist himself, has produced with his labour. Even if we assume that the original investment in the capitalist's business had been the capitalist's rightful and fairly acquired property, the expansive logic of capitalism requires that the capitalist always reinvests part of the profit. Some of it has to go to raw materials once again, and some will go for the wages of the additional workers whom the capitalist will employ. In their case, the capitalist is not just appropriating for himself the surplus value that their labour produces; he is also paying the wages with surplus value – the unpaid labour of other workers. So even if the workers are paid a fair wage for their labour, the 'whole thing still remains the age-old activity of the conqueror, who buys commodities from the conquered with the money he has stolen from them' (p. 728). The full extent of the exploitation of workers thus becomes visible only when we do not focus solely on an individual worker or a particular factory, but on the whole class of workers – the *proletariat*. Capital then appears in its true guise, not as a thing, but as a social relation between two classes of people, which is mediated through things.

In contrast to his detailed analysis of the essential logic of capitalism, Marx had relatively little to say about the alternative: a communist society. A key communist demand was that the means of production have to be socialized: the productive resources and material assets have to be the property of the community as a whole. Whereas liberal egalitarian theories such as Rawls's rely on the idea of private ownership of property, but attempt to compensate for its inequalities through fair schemas of redistribution, communists advocate a more radical idea of justice in which private property itself is inherently unjust. They claim that, if all we do is redistribute income from those who own the means of production to those who do not, then we have not transformed the conditions that make exploitation possible and redistribution necessary. Hence, abolishing private property ownership has to be an essential step.

As we know, the attempts to realize such a society have not fared well. The relationship between Marx's thought and the ideological system referred to as 'Marxism' continues to be debated, as does his legacy in communist dictatorships. Yet the problems of capitalism he so sharply exposed have not disappeared. Child labour and life-threatening working conditions may have been eradicated from British cities, but child labourers continue to risk their lives in the shipbreaking yards and sweatshops of Bangladesh. Even though we have witnessed a dramatic increase in wealth through the expansion and intensification of capitalism, we have also seen its increasingly uneven distribution globally. Marx reminds us that the cheap commodities that we pick up from supermarket shelves do not appear out of thin air, but that specific conditions made their production possible. Although we would often prefer not to know about these conditions – the exploitation of workers, the use of child labour, animal cruelty and environmental devastation – the exposure of such conditions must be an important step that leads to political transformation.

▶ Anarchist alternatives

Abolition of private property was also a central aim of another radical political movement, which emerged concurrently with communism – anarchism. Marx's interlocutor and opponent, Pierre-Joseph Proudhon (1809–65), famously declared that property was theft. The seminal thinkers of anarchism, such as Proudhon and Michael Bakunin (1814–70), shared with Marx many of the same critical insights about liberalism.

Liberalism endorses formal equality in the form of equal opportunities and equal political rights, but it ignores material inequalities, the unequal access to resources. The political ideals of freedom and equality thus have to be connected with issues of economic equity in order to mean anything; otherwise, formal political rights may function only as a pretty façade that hides devastating poverty. However, despite their common roots in working-class activism and in the critique of liberalism, anarchists and communists soon fell into bitter disagreements, and rivalries surfaced.

The issue that most strongly divided the two movements was whether or not to participate in parliamentary politics. The followers of Marx supported the idea of forming workers' parties. They believed that it was necessary to be involved in the existing political processes while preparing for the seizure of power in revolution, and they started to organize into parties towards the end of the nineteenth century. For the anarchists, this was a faulty strategy. In the words of the Italian anarchist Errico Malatesta, it would only 'lead the masses back to slavery' (Malatesta, *Life and Ideas*, p. 158). Any form of government, even a socialist or a communist one, implied a centralized, hierarchical decision-making apparatus, and it was naive to believe that this new government would not create a new form of oppression. Anarchists insisted that popular revolution had to abolish the state; this could not be accomplished by submitting to its rules, namely the procedures of parliamentary politics.

After the Russian Revolution in 1917 and the creation of the Soviet state, twentieth-century anarchist movements emphasized their distinctiveness even more strongly and divided into separate strands, such as anarcho-syndicalists, eco-anarchists, anarcha-feminists and anarcho-libertarians. The core idea that unites all of these various strands continues to be the rejection of the state: the state is not only unnecessary; it is also detrimental to people's moral integrity and wellbeing. Anarchists advocate instead forms of governance such as communes and associations that are as local and close to the direct control of the people as possible.

Anarchists thus disagree with the Hobbesian claim that the abolition of the state would only lead to something worse, such as a war of all against all. Despite the common meaning of 'anarchy', the goal of anarchists is not chaos or violent disorder. Rather, their answer to the fundamental question of political philosophy – can people co-operate in the absence of imposed rules and authority? – is an unequivocal yes. Groups and societies are capable of effective and harmonious self-organization when given the chance. Anarchists claim, however, that in a centralized state all social experimentation, local initiative and self-directed activities are discouraged or forbidden outright. Anarchists also remind us that the security that the state provides is essentially based on its monopoly on violence. Citizens must submit to this regime of organized violence in return for their civil rights. Like Marx, anarchists argue that state violence, or its threat, is supposedly only used to protect rights, but in fact it is an effective means of establishing and upholding deep inequalities.

The influence of anarchism is visible today in numerous contemporary campaigns and protest movements such as anti-globalization and the Occupy movements, which are organized on the principles of self-government, non-hierarchy and decentralization. Many contemporary anarchists do not support the idea of a violent revolutionary overthrow of the state; they argue instead that we should develop new networks and institutions within the state. However, anarchists continue to eschew party politics and instead experiment with other ways of promoting social change: for example, by organizing communal gardens, food co-operatives, block parties, neighbourhood services or alternative economies. Many activists see anarchism today as a vast umbrella movement or a countercultural lifestyle challenging the brutality and conformity of consumer capitalism.

The nation-state as 'fiction'

The state has historically evolved from an instrument of domination and security to a complex provider of services. Even if many people today take for granted its existence and the services that it provides, it is worth remembering that the autonomous nation-state as we know it is not a natural or self-evident form of political organization, but a relatively recent invention in political history. The political theorist Benedict Anderson, for example, has described the nation-state as 'an imagined political community' – its existence in fact requires a collective act of imagination (Anderson, *Imagined Communities,* 1991). In contrast to such face-to-face communities as a family or the residents of a particular town, citizens of a nation-state must learn to imagine themselves as belonging to a nation with fixed borders and strict requirements for citizenship.

The idea that the sovereign nation-state could be abolished and replaced with some other kind of political organization is thus not an impossible idea. Some political theorists are, in fact, predicting the disappearance of the nation-state as the inevitable consequence of globalization. They argue that we are undergoing an upheaval comparable to the profound political transformation that accompanied the emergence of nation-states out of the mosaic of principalities and trading cities in the Middle Ages. Now, however, the process signals the death and not the birth of the state. Economic globalization has meant that individual nation-states have already largely lost their power to make independent economic decisions, to rein in the markets or to ameliorate their detrimental effects on citizens. It is also increasingly difficult to secure their borders and control the flows of people, goods and information across those borders. The critical question of the necessity and political future of the state, posed by anarchists, is thus perhaps more acute today than ever before.

9

The traumas and promises of twentieth-century politics

'We do not know [...] how many of the normal people around us would be willing to accept the totalitarian way of life. [...] It is easy to realize the extent to which totalitarian propaganda and even some totalitarian institutions answer the needs of the new homeless masses, but it is almost impossible to know how many of them, if they are further exposed to a constant threat of unemployment, will gladly acquiesce to a 'population policy' that consists of regular elimination of surplus people, and how many, once they have fully grasped their growing incapacity to bear the burdens of modern life, will gladly conform to a system that, together with spontaneity, eliminates responsibility.'

Arendt, *The Origins of Totalitarianism*, p. 437

The twentieth century brought many of the political ideas discussed so far to fruition and spread them across the globe: parliamentary democracy, universal suffrage, advanced capitalism, liberalism and social welfare came to frame our political debates and everyday lives. The twentieth century also introduced some new and unparalleled political ideas and phenomena. I have selected two for closer scrutiny in this chapter: totalitarianism and feminism. These phenomena have not only dramatically changed the lives of millions of people worldwide, but they have also challenged some of the central ideas of political philosophy itself.

▶ The 'atomized' society: totalitarianism

Totalitarianism can be characterized as a form of tyranny, a political system in which a single person, faction or class rules with unlimited power. It is nevertheless important to recognize the distinctiveness of totalitarianism as a specifically modern phenomenon, one that combined unprecedented coercion with an all-embracing secular ideology. In her monumental work *The Origins of Totalitarianism* (1951), Hannah Arendt (1906–75), a Jew originally from Germany and one of the foremost political thinkers of the twentieth century, emphasizes the 'horrible originality' of totalitarianism. She insists that the dictatorship of National Socialism after 1938 and the dictatorship of Bolshevism after 1930 were new political formations, and not merely updated versions of tyranny, despotism or dictatorship. These totalitarian regimes developed entirely new political institutions and practices and destroyed all the existing social, legal and political traditions as well.

Arendt's chief claim is that totalitarianism is a particularly modern phenomenon because its primary condition is an atomized mass society: isolated individuals who have no strong ties to communities and who are indifferent to shared political goals. She acknowledges that the breakdown of traditional social hierarchies brought us political equality, but modern society also came to be distinguished by competition and concomitant loneliness. The experience of being totally superfluous became a mass phenomenon. 'What prepares men for totalitarian domination in the non-totalitarian world is the fact that loneliness, once a borderline experience usually suffered in certain marginal conditions like old age, has become an everyday experience' (p. 317). Isolated, superfluous and lonely people found the totalitarian promise of belonging to a movement irresistible.

Totalitarian regimes thus depend on isolated people, but they also deliberately attempt to destroy all social and family ties to deepen such isolation. In Stalin's Soviet state the device of 'guilt by association', for example, meant that not only the defendant but also all the people related to him, from mere acquaintances up to his closest friends and relatives, became victims of state purges. As soon as a person was accused, his friends were turned into his enemies, forced to forego all contact with him in order to save themselves. Ultimately, it was best, as a precaution, to avoid all intimate contact as far as possible.

The feature that is often puzzling about totalitarian regimes is their total disregard for all utilitarian or economic concerns: they will employ and develop costly mechanisms for exterminating or deporting scores of their own people at times when a war effort, for example, would seem to require the opposite – more soldiers and workers. Arendt argues that there is a logic to their operation. Totalitarian ideology is not based on narrow nationalist, military or economic interests, as we often assume. Rather, it is essentially based on the idea that there are inevitable, ironclad laws – the Laws of History in the case of Stalin's Soviet Union, or the Laws of Nature in Hitler's Nazi Germany – that determine the destiny of a people, a higher goal towards which all events and actions, even the seemingly most absurd, inevitably lead. The Leader must be obeyed unconditionally, not because he is particularly just or wise, but because he is charged with the mission of implementing the historical or natural laws. Such an all-encompassing ideology also absolves individuals of all responsibility for their individual actions, no matter how horrendous or seemingly irrational those actions may be.

Totalitarian regimes are thus never content simply to rule by external means, such as the state's machinery of violence. They need people to believe in them, and therefore they need propaganda. Arendt argues that totalitarian propaganda is intimately linked to terror, however, because totalitarian regimes are not content just to fabricate lies. Instead, they will shape reality so that it corresponds to the lie – after which the lie ceases to be a lie. Totalitarian regimes will not just assert, for example, that no opposition to the regime exists, nor is it enough to kill all opponents; the regime will also meticulously erase all traces that such people *ever* existed. This quest for consistency leaves no possibility for martyrdom, grief, mourning or remembrance because there are no witnesses or testimonies; there is no shared, social meaning that can be allotted to the horrors. Instead, the regime creates organized oblivion, a completely fictitious world that is logical, consistent and well organized – a world in which the uprooted can feel safe. Eventually, the fictitious quality of the everyday world makes propaganda largely superfluous.

> *Given the possibility to exterminate Jews like bedbugs, namely by poison gas, it is no longer necessary to propagate that Jews are bedbugs; given the power to teach a whole nation the history of the Russian evolution without mentioning the name Trotsky, there is no further need for propaganda against Trotsky. (pp. 413–14).*

Arendt's fundamental, and shocking, insight is that the completely fictitious world of totalitarianism ultimately reveals to us that factuality itself depends upon the existence of a non-totalitarian world in which we can make real distinctions between truths and lies. The ideal subject of totalitarianism is thus not the convinced Nazi or the convinced communist, but anyone who has lost the ability to make distinctions between fact and fiction and between true and false.

Whether totalitarianism as a political phenomenon is something that will stay with us or a fleeting episode in political history remains to be seen. North Korea would certainly meet Arendt's criteria for a totalitarian regime, but we can detect totalitarian characteristics in many other current political systems as well.

The 'Third Wave' experiment

When we assess the legacy of totalitarianism, it is worth keeping in mind the notorious 'Third Wave' class experiment conducted in 1967 in Palo Alto, California. History teacher Ron Jones conducted an experiment with his class of 15-year-olds to study the rise of the Nazis in Germany before the Second World War. His students, like many of us, had found it difficult to understand the attraction of such a movement and the German peoples' seemingly blind loyalty to it. So the teacher created a fictitious movement in the classroom called 'The Third Wave'. He himself was its authoritarian leader and the movement had its own beliefs, rules, flag, salute and membership cards. To his surprise, the majority of the students became completely devoted to the movement, and rapidly the experiment got out of control. In a matter of days, the students turned into aggressive zealots attempting to convert others to the movement and enforcing its rules through bullying and threatening behaviour. Hence, we should not harbour the comforting illusion that totalitarian movements could never rise to power in our societies. In order to detect signs of totalitarianism in our own political systems, as well as to prevent its horrors from recurring, it is crucial that we understand its rationality and the political conditions for its possibility.

▶ The feminist revolution

I want to finish this chapter by focusing on another, very different kind of political mass movement, a non-violent 'revolution' that has reverberated across the globe and profoundly changed our societies and our way of life in the twentieth century – feminism. Feminism is generally defined as a social and political movement that advocates equal political and economic opportunities and rights for women. It is arguably the most lasting and influential of modern social movements: during the twentieth century billions of women have entered the realm of institutional politics as legitimate and active participants, first as voters, and then, increasingly, as politicians.

The significance of feminism cannot be reduced merely to a numerical increase in women's political participation. More fundamentally, it forces us to reconsider many of the ideas essential to organizing a canon of political philosophy. Until fairly recently, almost all political philosophers defended the view that there was a natural foundation for men's and women's different roles in society: the restrictions on women's political and civil rights, education and career opportunities were justified by the argument that women were naturally unsuited to or incapable of taking part in the political and economic activities in the public sphere. The power relations between the genders were thus not recognized as a political phenomenon, but were simply assumed to be natural. This blindness of political philosophers to one of the most common instances of oppressive power relations facing them has inevitably had serious consequences for many of the founding ideas of our political tradition.

Here let us briefly return to the story of the social contract. As we saw in Chapter 4, this influential story tells how a new political society was created through an original contract. It is a revolutionary tale of the natural freedom and equality of all people, the emancipatory doctrine *par excellence*, hailing universal freedom as the guiding principle of the modern era. Yet the contract did not include freedom for women.

▲ The 'rediscovery' of early feminist thinkers such as Mary Wollstonecraft (pictured here) and Mary Astell has enabled us to see the degree to which political philosophy has been shaped by and for men.

The political philosopher Carole Pateman (1940–) argues that only half of that story is ever told: standard commentaries usually do not mention that women were excluded from the contract. She notes how the naturally free and equal individuals who people the pages written by social contract theorists are a disparate collection, covering 'the spectrum of Rousseau's social beings to Hobbes' entities reduced to matter in motion', but what they have in common is that they are all male (Pateman, *The Sexual Contract*, p. 41). In other words, the theory states that, if relations of subordination between *men* are to be legitimate, they must originate in a contract. Women were not party to the contract, they are subject to it: the contract established not only men's political freedom, but also their political right over women and their bodies. Mary Astell, a contemporary of Locke and an early feminist writer, asked sarcastically: 'if all Men are born Free, how is it that all women are born Slaves?' (Astell, *Political Writings*, p. 18). Until late into the nineteenth century the legal and civil position of a wife resembled that of a slave. Like a slave, she was her husband's possession in the sense that she had no independent legal existence apart from him, and he was also entitled to punish her physically.

Pateman argues that the significance of this position is not limited to a bit of poor philosophical reasoning by philosophers long dead. The structures of our society and our everyday lives still incorporate features of a patriarchal conception of marriage and family. Husbands obviously no longer enjoy the extensive rights over their wives that they still possessed in the mid-nineteenth century. However, aspects of conjugal subjection linger on, both in cultural attitudes, and in the legal jurisdictions of the many countries that refuse to admit that rape is possible within marriage, for example.

Feminist political thought also has a conflicted relationship with liberalism. On the one hand, feminism relies historically and theoretically on the liberal principles of individual autonomy and equal opportunity: mainstream feminism has largely taken the form of eliminating types of gender discrimination by removing legal barriers to women's full participation in public life and by safeguarding women's right to exercise fully their bodily autonomy. At the same time, feminist political theorists have also revealed that many of the central ideas and conceptual distinctions that organize liberalism are deeply problematic.

Feminism v. individualism

Feminist political thinkers such as Wendy Brown (1955–) have questioned the fundamental liberal understanding of the individual as autonomous, independent and self-interested. Women are understood as being very different from what this model suggests, and they are brought up to be very different: they are expected to suppress their egotistical interests and demonstrate caring and nurturing qualities. Early feminist demands for political rights were often repudiated on the grounds that women did not have any interests separate from those of their husbands and fathers, and therefore they had no need for political representation. Even if women have now had equal political rights for nearly a century, the idea that all their actions are driven by calculated self-interest has been significantly absent from our society centred on families. Family has been understood as natural and women's traditional role in it has been to surrender their self-interest so that their husbands and children can attain their independence and become autonomous liberal individuals. Brown points out that this 'naturalization of families means that women simply cannot be the possessive individualists men are' (Brown, *States of Injury*, p. 148). While holding that all people are autonomous individualists, the liberal political order in fact relies on women being selfless and caring nurturers of family values.

The liberal focus on equal opportunities has also proven problematic for many feminist political goals. When we assert that men and women should have equal opportunities, do we mean that they should be treated exactly the same? Most feminists would claim that equality does not mean this. Rather, it requires that we take into account women's specific circumstances, for example the fact that women can bear children. If we outlaw forms of gender discrimination in the workplace, but define paying jobs in such a way as to make them inaccessible to people with children, then we cannot claim that we have achieved gender equality. Hence, in addition to anti-discrimination laws, we need more radical political changes such as parental leaves for both genders and affordable nurseries if we really want to ensure that women have opportunities equal to men in terms of career prospects. In the current situation in which women do the majority of domestic work and childcare, women are inevitably concentrated in low-paying, part-time jobs or remain economically dependent on their husbands. Too often, women today still face a choice between family and career, a choice that men seldom have to make.

The liberal vocabulary of personal freedom and choice also often effectively masks the systemic aspects of sexism. The measure of women's liberation is understood to be the individual choices that they are able to make: to become executives or housewives, to have white weddings or to buy pornography. Power is often understood simply as another thing women can choose. Within this framework the fact that many women choose to stay at home or opt out of more demanding and higher-paying employment opportunities is understood straightforwardly as their own free choice. The impediments to their social and political success are understood as personal or psychological rather than political. The problem with the excessive focus on choice is that women have to make their choices in a society of unequal power relations. These unequal power relations restrict their possibilities and options, but also profoundly shape and construct the kinds of beings they become. In other words, women's self-understanding, their desires, ambitions and preferences necessarily take a different shape in a sexist society than in a society that is gender equal.

Hence, despite the fact that our societies have adopted a variety of legal and political mechanisms intended to ensure gender equality, we still have a long way to go. Whether we read statistics concerning violence against women, study the widening gap between women and men caught in the cycle of poverty, or analyse the gender of political and corporate elites, it is evident that gender equality is still a distant goal. It is my contention that political philosophy must play a crucial role in the on-going critical reassessment of gender. Women's political oppression cannot be eradicated exclusively through legal measures because it is largely the result of tacit cultural norms, beliefs and attitudes, as well as everyday habits and practices ranging from child rearing to advertising. Political philosophy must submit these beliefs and practices to critical scrutiny. This is important, not only for the achievement of gender equality but also for the attainment of a better political philosophy.

In sum, feminist political philosophy should be understood as a critical current within political philosophy. Feminist political philosophy reworks political philosophy from the inside and challenges us to reconsider the question with which this book began: What is political philosophy? As the feminist slogan 'the personal is political' implies, political philosophy cannot be limited to a study of what happens in the institutions of government, but must concern our everyday lives and the power relations between different individuals and groups within the 'private realm'. Feminism reminds us to be wary of all attempts to define the 'legitimate' or 'real' political questions. As we have seen, such attempts have often functioned as political acts themselves, rendering some power relations and forms of oppression completely invisible.

Epilogue: What next?

Today we are faced with enormous political challenges. Economic growth has lifted millions of people out of poverty, but its fruits have been divided very unevenly. According to current estimates, around one billion people suffer from starvation, while the richest 10 per cent of the world's adults own 85 per cent of all global assets. Economic growth has also created huge environmental problems: if the current trends of both economic growth and population growth continue, by 2050 we will need at least four planets' worth of natural resources. Human-induced climate change is perhaps our most immanent environmental problem: millions of people are going to suffer hunger, water shortages, diseases and catastrophic coastal flooding if we do not put a stop to climate change.

Many people are trying to respond to these problems with scientific and technological innovations. It has been suggested, for example, that we could tackle climate change with geo-engineering – large-scale manipulations of the earth, such as spraying sulphate aerosols into the stratosphere to alter the reflectivity of the planet or fertilizing the ocean with iron to spur blooms of carbon-sucking plankton. Such technologies are extremely risky, however, and some thinkers, such as Matthew Liao, an American bioethicist, have suggested that such measures should be combined with less dangerous technologies of human engineering. We could solve the problem of climate change by the biomedical modification of humans to make us better at mitigating and adapting to its effects. Liao's suggestions include artificially introducing mild intolerance to red meat by stimulating the immune system against common bovine proteins and reducing our ecological footprint by reducing the size of human beings. This could be done by using pre-implantation genetic diagnosis to select shorter embryos or by introducing voluntary hormone treatments to tall children (Liao, 'Hand-made humans...').

Irrespective of what you think of these undeniably innovative suggestions, their highly controversial nature should make it apparent that science and technology alone cannot solve the problems we face. We need politics: political debate and decisions on the desired ends and acceptable means by which our societies and ways of life should be changed. Engaging in such a political project is vital, not just for politicians and political theorists, but for all of us.

The alarming situation is not helped by the fact that many of our vital political challenges require *global* solutions. The future of humanity as well as of our planet itself has become dependent on events and processes such as climate change that are currently beyond any single nation's control. Globalization thus seems to call for some form of global governance as its necessary counterpart.

What form this global governance could and should take poses a difficult question. The variety of forms of political organization created in human history is bewildering, but never before has there been a form of governance that had both a global reach and was based on anything resembling modern democratic principles. A crucial question for political philosophy today must therefore be: Can democracy, even in principle, be extended beyond individual nation-states to a global level? Is the global democracy project – the democratization of the international community, a process joining together states with different political traditions and at various stages of development – a viable political objective?

As we saw earlier, Kant was already arguing for a cosmopolitan political order in the eighteenth century. Following him, political philosophers have presented numerous plans for democratically organized leagues of nations, world federations, cosmopolitan democracies and other combinations of representative and international governance. However, many political philosophers have also dismissed outright the idea that a democratically legitimated cosmopolitan order supported by a sense of identification and solidarity with humanity as a whole could even exist. They argue that it would be impossible in principle – it is a metaphysical, rather than a merely practical, impossibility.

A decisive question concerns political identity. Critics have argued that a global *demos* would require a shared global identity. Such an identity is not only currently lacking, but also is impossible, in principle, because identity always requires difference: every collective identity needs some external other in contrast to which it can define itself. Hence, there can never be a democracy of humankind, only democracies of particular collectives such as nations. A second, powerful line of objection is connected with critics' understanding of the essential nature of politics. They claim that, because politics is fundamentally about power, the only possibility for world peace must lie in a balance between roughly equal centres of power. Any global government would necessarily become a tool in the hands of the most powerful national governments: if such a project were ever realized, it would signify that one dominant power had been able to impose its interests and conception of the world on the entire planet.

Third, the impossibility of a global political order is often connected with the nature of democracy itself. It has been argued that democracy is possible only in communities of moderate size. The world is too large, in principle, to allow the establishment of democratic institutions because the opportunities available for ordinary citizens to participate in such institutions would diminish to the vanishing point. A world government or confederation of states would have to work through elected representatives, each representing millions of people, and such a system could no longer meaningfully be called democratic.

The supporters of global democracy have responded by acknowledging that collective identities are often formed in contrast to, and even in conflict with, an actually existing other. But they claim that there seems to be no reason in principle why the difference required for identity could not also be difference from an imagined or past historical collective identity, for example an identity from which one wishes to mark one's distance. Arash Abizadeh, for example, has suggested that, although one way to construct European identity is to ground it in a Christian-based identity defined in sharp contrast to Europe's Islamic frontiers, a second way would be to construct identity in terms of the political values and institutions of human rights, religious tolerance and political freedom, which seem to have become increasingly entrenched in Europe since the end of the Second World War. 'The contrast, in the second case, might be with Europe's own history, and with a lingering past that it seeks to leave behind' (Abizadeh, 'Collective Identity', p. 58). Similarly, for a cosmopolitan identity, 'humanity's own past provides a rich and terrifying repository in contrast to which it could constitute its difference' (p. 58).

The supporters of global democracy have also argued that, even if we accept that politics is fundamentally about power, the further problem of how power relations can be regulated and controlled democratically is not specific to global democracy. Democracy, no matter what its scale, always requires adequate mechanisms and principles such as power sharing and minority rights so as not to degenerate into tyranny. In other words, if a functioning democracy is possible at all, on any level, then there is no metaphysical reason why it would not be possible on a global level as well. Some political thinkers have also insisted that a necessary condition for global democracy is the development of a global and pluralist security community – a group of collectives that have become so deeply integrated that they do not prepare for the use of political violence against each other because they have learned to resolve conflicts by means of peaceful changes. Such a pluralist security community does not require a unitary global government or military.

The size of the community does not have to be a decisive issue, as long as we understand cosmopolitan democracy, not as a single political institution such as a world parliament, but as a *multileveled* process of global democratization. Such a process is not only possible; it is an already existing, widely shared political project that can and should be continuously improved and enriched. Global democratization could mean developing the *transformative* possibilities of existing global organizations such as the UN, the WTO and the international judicial institutions, for example. There exist various concrete proposals for the democratic reform of the UN – its funding could be reorganized, the power of the General Assembly could be strengthened, a new Parliamentary Assembly established, the Security Council's permanent members' power to veto could be abolished and so on. There are also innovative new ideas for empowering global civil society and for creating completely new institutional arrangements such as a Global Truth Commission.

Many political thinkers also emphasize the central importance of fair trade for the process of global democratization. The democratization of such existing institutions as the IMF, World Bank and WTO, as well as the creation of new organizations such as an international debt arbitration mechanism and a global tax organization, would make heavily indebted poor countries less dependent on global finance and on the self-seeking interests of their debtors. This would strengthen their sovereignty and, consequently, their potential to make economic policy decisions democratically. The critical assessments of global democratic governance must thus be based on many different criteria, not only on adequate electoral representation. We also have to consider whether and to what extent global practices of governance are able to meet the principles of accountability, fairness and transparency.

We should also remember that in politics there are seldom any perfect solutions. In any global democratic system, regardless of the form it takes, the possibilities of a single citizen influencing global decisions will be miniscule. Nevertheless, such possibilities might be considerably greater than they would be given the alternatives, such as if the direction of globalization were decided solely by free markets or by military might.

While historically the emergence of functioning democracies has often been a difficult and unlikely process, the attempts to identify universally valid necessary conditions for democratic transitions have not been particularly successful either. Democracies have developed and survived in vastly different and adverse conditions. Democracy in India, for example, is often given as an example of a system that contradicts all the assumed necessary conditions for its emergence. There, democracy has grown and survived in the context of very high levels of cultural heterogeneity and economic inequality, low per-capita income and enormous population size (Koenig-Archibugi, 'Is Global Democracy Possible?'). If the process of democracy has managed to overcome a myriad of seemingly impossible obstacles within individual states, this suggests that it should be possible for it to do so at the transnational level as well.

Given the complexity of the issues involved, I am obviously not going to try and solve the problem of democratic global governance here. But before giving up the idea as an impossible dream, I would like to issue the warning that, in politics, it is always risky to declare that something is impossible. Rather, it is worth keeping in mind that politics is a realm in which just about anything is possible – a realm capable of surprising optimists, pessimists and realists alike. And personally I believe that it is precisely the unpredictability of politics, as opposed to the certainty of religion or science, that must sustain our hopes for a better world.

This 100 ideas section gives ways you can explore the subject in more depth. It's much more than just the usual reading list.

100 IDEAS

Ten works by philosophers discussed in this book

Ten classics that had to be excluded from this book

Five introductions to political philosophy

Five webpages

Five podcasts

Five political philosophy journals

Ten contemporary political philosophers who had to be excluded from this book

46 **Martha Nussbaum** American philosopher and classicist who has most recently focused on ideas of global justice

47 **Jacques Rancière** French Marxist thinker

48 **Charles Taylor** Canadian philosopher associated with the communitarian critique of the liberal notion of the 'self'

49 **Cornel West** American thinker who looks, especially, at the effects of race, class and gender in the United States

50 **Slavoj Žižek** Slovene critic of neoliberalism and advocate of socialism

Five novels

51 *Robinson Crusoe* (1719) by Daniel Defoe

52 *The Trial* (1925) by Franz Kafka

53 *Brave New World* (1932) by Aldous Huxley

54 *Animal Farm* (1945) by George Orwell

55 *Lord of the Flies* (1954) by William Golding

Five films

56 *Modern Times* (directed by Charlie Chaplin, 1936)

57 *The Battle of Algiers* (directed by Gillo Pontecorvo, 1966)

58 *Dogville* (directed by Lars von Trier, 2003)

59 *4 Months, 3 Weeks and 2 Days* (directed by Cristian Mungiu, 2007)

60 *Persepolis* (animated film by Marjane Satrapi, 2007)

Five songs

61 'The Internationale' (composed by Pierre De Geyter in 1888; new English lyrics by Billy Bragg)

62 'Strange Fruit' (1939) by Billie Holliday

63 'We Shall Overcome' (published in 1947, original gospel song composed by Charles Albert Tindley)

64 'Imagine' (1971) by John Lennon

65 'Anarchy in the U.K.' (1976) by the Sex Pistols

Five artworks

66 *The Third of May 1808* (1814) by Francisco Goya

67 *Liberty Leading the People* (1830) by Eugène Delacroix

68 *Guernica* (1937) by Pablo Picasso

69 *Your body is a battleground* (1989) by Barbara Kruger

70 *250 cm line tattooed on 6 paid people* (1999) by Santiago Sierra

Ten political 'isms'

71 Anarchism Political theory and practice advocating the abolition of the state; in modern times first developed as a consistent set of ideas by William Godwin and Pierre-Joseph Prudhon

72 Socialism Political doctrine whereby the means of production (factories, farms and so on) are owned by society, whether this means by the state, the 'people' or cooperatively; in Marxist thought, the transitional stage before communism

73 Communism In Marxist thought, the ultimate development of society as the state falls away leaving a classless, money-less society in which the means of production are collectively owned and wealth is distributed according to need

Advocacy of a classless, money-less society in which the means of production belongs to the community; in Marxist thought, the final stage in the revolutionary struggle in which the proletariat is victorious and such a society is established

74 Liberalism Political doctrine based on the ideals of liberty and equality, variously comprising ideas such as civil rights, free and fair elections, private property and free trade

75 Conservatism The belief that politics should preserve traditional values and institutions

76 Feminism A diverse set of ideas, beliefs, movements and agendas for action that seeks to establish male – female equality in terms of social, political and economic rights and opportunities

77 Environmentalism A broad philosophy, ideology and social movement that advocates the protection of the natural world

78 Cosmopolitanism The belief that all human ethnic groups have equal worth and status

79 Pluralism The acknowledgement of a diversity of political systems and of their validity; also the belief that there should be multiple centres of power in a society

80 Egalitarianism The belief that all human beings have equal worth and status

Five schools of political philosophy

81 **Liberalism** School of political philosophy derived from number 74

82 **Libertarianism** Political school that advocates liberty, or freedom, as the highest political goal and which aims to reduce the role of the state as far as possible

83 **Communitarianism** Political philosophy that emphasizes the role of the community in defining and shaping individuals

84 **Utilitarianism** Political school that, following the ideas of Jeremy Bentham, holds that society should be governed in such a way as to promote the maximum happiness of the maximum number of people

85 **Marxism** School of political thought that takes the ideas of Karl Marx as its basis, although in practice the interpretation of such ideas has proved diverse; see also numbers 72 and 73

Five constitutions (modern)

86 **Presidential republic**

87 **Parliamentary republic**

88 **Constitutional monarchy**

89 **Absolute monarchy**

90 **Single-party state**

Six constitutions (ancient, according to Aristotle)

91 **Royalty**

92 **Tyranny**

Four anecdotes

97 Thomas Carlyle, an eminent Scottish writer, was allegedly scolded by a businessman at a dinner party for endlessly talking about books: 'Ideas, Mr Carlyle, ideas – nothing but ideas.' Carlyle's rejoinder was: 'There was once a man called Rousseau who wrote a book containing nothing but ideas. The second edition was bound in the skins of those who laughed at the first.'

98 Mahatma Gandhi, one of the greatest political philosophers of the twentieth century, was asked by a reporter: 'Mr Gandhi, what do you think of Western civilization?' Gandhi's unforgettable one-liner was: 'I think it would be a good idea!'

99 When you next want to complain about the problems of democracy it is worth remembering Winston Churchill's famous words in his House of Commons speech in 1947: 'Democracy is the worst form of government, except for all those other forms that have been tried from time to time.'

100 Diogenes of Sinope, one of the founders of Cynic philosophy, was relaxing in the sunlight, when Alexander the Great, a powerful king, happened to come by. Excited to meet the famous philosopher, Alexander asked if there was any favour he might do for him. Diogenes replied, 'Yes, stand out of my sunlight.' The anecdote illustrates well the central tenet of his philosophy: the total disregard for wealth and prestige.

ALL THAT MATTERS: POLITICAL PHILOSOPHY

References

Arash Abizadeh, 'Does Collective Identity Presuppose an Other? On the Alleged Incoherence of Global Solidarity', *American Political Science Review* 99/1 (2005): 45–60.

Benedict Anderson, *Imagined Communities: Reflections on the Origin and Spread of Nationalism* (London: Verso, 1991).

Hannah Arendt, *The Origins of Totalitarianism* (San Diego: Harcourt, 1968).

Aristotle, *Politics*, trans. T.A. Sinclair (London: Penguin, 1981).

Mary Astell, *Political Writings*, ed. Patricia Springborg (Cambridge: Cambridge University Press, 1996).

Wendy Brown, *States of Injury* (Princeton: Princeton University Press, 1995).

Friedrich Hayek, *The Road to Serfdom* (London: Routledge, 1944).

Thomas Hobbes, *Leviathan* (New York: Barnes & Noble, 2004).

Max Horkheimer and Theodor Adorno, *Dialectic of Enlightenment*, trans. John Cumming (New York: Continuum, 2000).

Immanuel Kant, *Political Writings*, ed. Hans Reiss, trans. H.B. Nisbet (Cambridge: Cambridge University Press, 1991).

Mathias Koenig-Archibugi, 'Is Global Democracy Possible?', European Journal of International Relations 17/3 (2010): 530–31.

Matthew Liao, 'Hand-made humans may hold the key to saving the world', The Sydney Morning Herald, 30 September 2012 (available from: www.smh.com.au/technology/sci-tech/handmade-humans-may-hold-the-key-to-saving-the-world-20120929-26s1n.html).

John Locke, *Two Treatises of Government*, ed. Peter Laslett (Cambridge: Cambridge University Press, 1988).

Niccolò Machiavelli, *The Prince*, trans. George Bull (London: Penguin, 2004).

Errico Malatesta, *Life and Ideas*, ed. Vernon Richards (London: Freedom Press, 1977).

Karl Marx, *Capital*, vol. I, trans. Ben Fowkes (London: Penguin, 1990).

John Stuart Mill, *On Liberty*, ed. Gertrude Himmelfarb (London: Penguin, 1985).

Carol Pateman, *The Sexual Contract* (Cambridge: Polity Press, 1988).

Plato, *Republic*, trans. Robin Waterfield (Oxford: Oxford University Press, 1994).

John Rawls, *A Theory of Justice* (Cambridge, MA: Harvard University Press, 1971).

Jean-Jacques Rousseau, *Discourse on the Origin of Inequality*, trans. James Miller (Indianapolis: Hackett Publishing Company, 1992).

Lucius Annaeus Seneca, *The Stoic Philosophy of Seneca: Essays and Letters of Seneca*, trans. Moses Hadas (New York: Random House, 1958).

Adam Smith, *Wealth of Nations*, ed. Charles J. Bullock (New York: Cosimo, 2007).

James Tully, *An Approach to Political Philosophy: Locke in Contexts* (Cambridge: Cambridge University Press, 1993).

ALL THAT MATTERS: POLITICAL PHILOSOPHY

Index

Acknowledgements

The author and publisher give their thanks for permission to reproduce the following images:

Chapter 2 The Pynx, Athens © Dmitri Kessel/Time Life Pictures/Getty Images **Chapter 6** Concentration camp © posztos/Shuttercock.com **Chapter 8** Child labourers © C.WisHisSoc/Everett/Rex Features **Chapter 9** Mary Wollstonecraft CSU Archv/Everett/Rex Features

ALL THAT MATTERS: POLITICAL PHILOSOPHY